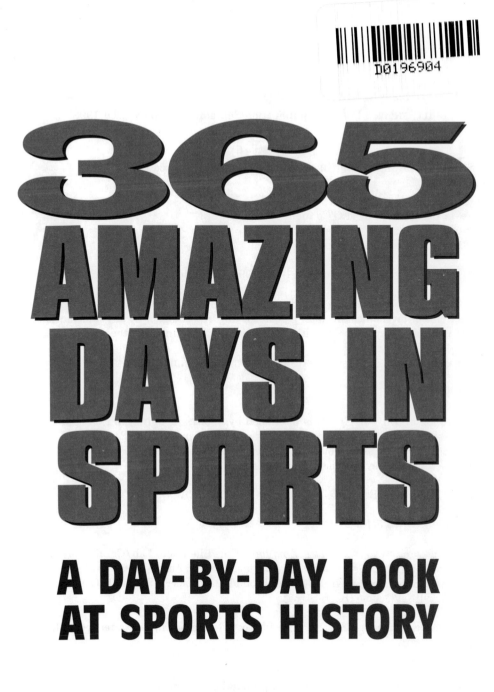

365 AMAZING DAYS IN SPORTS

A DAY-BY-DAY LOOK AT SPORTS HISTORY

By David Fischer

From the editors of SPORTS ILLUSTRATED FOR KIDS

365 Amazing Days in Sports

SPORTS ILLUSTRATED FOR KIDS publication/September 1995 (revised 1998)

SPORTS ILLUSTRATED FOR KIDS and are registered trademarks of Time Inc.

Cover design by Sheryl O'Connell
Interior design by Pegi Goodman
Illustrations by David Sheldon

For information, address: SPORTS ILLUSTRATED FOR KIDS

ISBN 1-886749-37-X

365 Amazing Days in Sports is published by SPORTS ILLUSTRATED FOR KIDS, a division of Time Inc. Its trademark is registered in the U.S. Patent and Trademark Office and in other countries. SPORTS ILLUSTRATED FOR KIDS, 1271 Avenue of the Americas, New York, NY 10020

PRINTED IN THE UNITED STATES OF AMERICA

CWO 10 9 8 7 6 5 4 3 2

Front cover photos *(clockwise, from top):* Time/Life Photo Lab (Cal Ripken), Richard Mackson/Sports Illustrated (Michael Jordan), Adrees Latiff/Reuters/Archive Photos (Brett Favre), Jed Jacobsohn/NBA/Allsport (Shaquille O'Neal), Paul J. Sutton/Duomo (Kerri Strug)

Back cover photos: AP/World Wide Photos (Florida Marlins); Walter Iooss, Jr. (Dwight Clark)

365 Amazing Days in Sports is a production of SPORTS ILLUSTRATED FOR KIDS Books: Cathrine Wolf, Editorial Director; Emily Petersen Perez, Art Director; Amy Lennard Goehner, Margaret Sieck, Senior Editors; Scott Gramling (Project Editor), Sherie Holder, Associate Editors

TABLE OF CONTENTS

INTRODUCTION

Pick a day, any day . . .

How about April 8? Well, on that day, in 1974, Hank Aaron cracked the 715th home run of his career and broke Babe Ruth's home run record!

How about November 21? Good choice. On that day, in 1969, the Seattle Mariners' Ken Griffey, Junior, was born.

What happened in sports on the day *you* were born? You can turn to the page with your birth date and find out!

365 Amazing Days in Sports tells you about many of the biggest moments in sports and when they happened. (There are two days on every page.) Find out when famous athletes celebrate *their* birthdays, and see more than 100 action-packed sports photos. Read about the greatest games, famous legends, and most exciting plays of all time.

You can start with January 1 and read straight through the year, one day at a time, or you can jump right to your birthday to find out what other exciting events happened on that special day. No matter where you start, one thing is for sure: This book will give you daily doses of amazing sports trivia to last the whole year long.

Was today an amazing day in sports? You bet. Flip to today's date in *365 Amazing Days in Sports,* and see for yourself!

JANUARY

January 26, 1997:
Brett Favre leads the
Packers to victory in
Super Bowl XXXI.

1

1929 In the Rose Bowl, California's Roy Riegels scooped up a fumble and ran toward his own end zone! A teammate tackled him near the goal line. The wrong-way run led to a 2-point safety, helping Georgia Tech win the game, 8–7.

1979 Notre Dame trailed Houston by 22 points with just 7 minutes, 37 seconds left in the Cotton Bowl. The Fighting Irish, led by quarterback Joe Montana, bounced back. They scored 23 points before the clock ran down and won the game, 35–34.

1993 The University of Miami was favored to win the Sugar Bowl (the Hurricanes had won 29 games in a row). But the University of Alabama exploded for 14 points in the third quarter. The 34–13 victory capped Alabama's perfect season and gave the Crimson Tide its first national title since 1979.

2

1965 Joe Namath, the University of Alabama star, became the richest rookie in football — or any other sport — today. He signed a $400,000 contract with the New York Jets. The quarterback, known as "Broadway Joe," turned the Jets from an average team into Super Bowl champs in just four years.

1994 In the NFL's regular-season finale, New England Patriot Drew Bledsoe threw a 36-yard touchdown pass to Michael Timpson to stun the Miami Dolphins in overtime, 33–27. The loss knocked Miami out of the playoffs.

1995 Tommie Frazier, the University of Nebraska's quarterback, wasn't scheduled to play in the Orange Bowl. But he came off the bench and engineered two fourth-quarter touchdowns. The Nebraska Cornhuskers beat the University of Miami Hurricanes, 24–17. Nebraska's final record was a perfect 13–0.

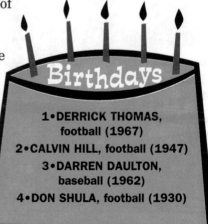

Birthdays

1•DERRICK THOMAS, football (1967)

2•CALVIN HILL, football (1947)

3•DARREN DAULTON, baseball (1962)

4•DON SHULA, football (1930)

JANUARY

3 **1983** Dallas Cowboy running back Tony Dorsett dashed 99 yards for a touchdown against the Minnesota Vikings. It was the longest run from scrimmage in NFL history! The record can be equaled but never broken.

1993 The Buffalo Bills mounted a major comeback in the AFC playoff wild-card game. In the third quarter, trailing the Houston Oilers, 35–3, the Bills scored 35 unanswered points! The Oilers tied the score with 12 seconds left, but Buffalo won in overtime, 41–38. No wonder it's called a *wild*-card game!

January 2, 1965: New York Jet Joe Namath becomes the richest rookie in sports.

1994 Steve Young of the San Francisco 49ers became the first NFL quarterback to win three straight passing titles. (Steve won the title, but the Philadelphia Eagles won today's game, 37–34.)

4 **1984** Wayne Gretzky became the first NHL player to score 8 or more points in a game twice in his career. He tallied four goals and four assists as the Edmonton Oilers downed the Minnesota North Stars, 12–8.

1996 The all-time winningest coach in the NFL called it quits. Don Shula had 347 career victories during his 33-season career with the Baltimore Colts and Miami Dolphins.

1997 The Jacksonville Jaguars pulled off one of the greatest post-season upsets in NFL history. Coming into the game, the Jaguars had a 14–19 record since entering the league as an expansion team in 1995. But they stunned the Denver Broncos, 30–27, and advanced to the AFC Championship Game.

JANUARY

5

1964 The San Diego Chargers lived up to their name in the American Football League championship game. They charged up and down the field against the Boston Patriots, gaining 610 yards in total offense. They pounded the Pats, 51–10.

1971 The Harlem Globetrotters were on a roll when they faced the New Jersey Reds. They had won 2,496 games in a row! New Jersey snapped the streak by beating the Globetrotters, 100–99.

1986 The Seattle SuperSonics were trailing the Phoenix Suns, 35–24, when the game was rained out! The roof in the Seattle Coliseum had sprung a leak. Officials postponed the game because of puddles on the floor.

6

1951 The longest game in NBA history finally came to an end after six overtimes. The game, between the Indianapolis Olympians and the Rochester Royals, lasted nearly four hours. Indianapolis finally won, 75–73.

1986 Six students at Cleveland State University, in Ohio, set out to bounce their way into *The Guinness Book of Records*. Taking turns, they began jumping up and down on a trampoline in the gym. Fifty-three exhausting days later, the six dizzy students stopped jumping. They had set the record.

1992 John McEnroe was named to the U.S. Davis Cup squad for a record 12th time. While representing the U.S. in Cup competition, John's career record has been 59–10.

1994 Nancy Kerrigan, the defending U.S. women's skating champion, was attacked on the eve of the U.S. Figure Skating Championships, in Detroit, Michigan. The attack injured her right knee and forced Nancy to withdraw from the competition.

Birthdays

5•TIM KERR, hockey (1960)
6•NANCY LOPEZ, golf (1957)
7•JEFF MONTGOMERY, baseball (1962)
8•WILLIE ANDERSON, basketball (1967)

**7**

1785 Jean Pierre Blanchard and J. Jeffries became the first men to travel between France and England in a hot-air balloon. The men had to throw everything out of the basket, including their clothes, to keep the balloon up in the air!

1980 The Minnesota North Stars defeated the Philadelphia Flyers, 7–1. The loss snapped Philly's unbeaten streak at 35 games. The Flyers had not lost a game since October 13.

January 5, 1971: The Harlem Globetrotters' 2,496-game winning streak is snapped.

1996 Talk about a shocker! The Indianapolis Colts, a wild-card entry, defeated the AFC West champion Kansas City Chiefs, 10–7, to reach the AFC Championship Game.

8

1945 Arkansas State University tied an NCAA record for the fewest points scored in a Division I basketball game today. ASU lost to the University of Kentucky Wildcats, 75–6.

1991 Rod Carew, who won seven American League batting titles between 1969 and 1978, was elected to baseball's Hall of Fame. Rod had a .328 lifetime batting average in 19 seasons with the Minnesota Twins and California Angels. His uniform number, 29, has been retired by both teams.

1994 With 55 seconds left in an NFL playoff game between the Green Bay Packers and the Detroit Lions, Packer quarterback Brett Favre threw a 40-yard touchdown pass to Sterling Sharpe. Green Bay won the game, 28–24.

1958 University of Cincinnati sophomore Oscar Robertson outscored the entire Seton Hall basketball team! The "Big O" poured in 56 points as the Bearcats beat the Pirates, 118–54.

1977 The Oakland Raiders scored on three straight possessions in the second quarter on their way to a 32–14 victory over Minnesota in Super Bowl XI. The loss was the Vikings' fourth in four Super Bowl appearances.

1988 The San Francisco 49ers had the NFL's best record, but they couldn't stop Anthony Carter. The Minnesota wide receiver caught 10 passes and set a playoff record with 227 receiving yards as the Vikings whipped the Niners, 36–24, to reach the championship game.

1979 High school basketball player Daryl Moreau of New Orleans went down in the record books when he hit his 126th free throw without a miss. In fact, it had been a year since he had missed a shot from the foul line.

1980 Boston Bruin rookie Jim Stewart played his first NHL game as goalie — and his last. Jim gave up three goals in the first four minutes of the game. He was soon sent to the bench and never played in the NHL again.

1982 San Francisco quarterback Joe Montana threw what seemed like an uncatchable pass to wide receiver Dwight Clark, who was in the end zone. Dwight made a spectacular grab for the touchdown. The TD and the extra point gave the 49ers a 28–27 win and sent them to their first Super Bowl.

1994 Dallas Cowboy running back Emmitt Smith, who won his third-straight rushing title, was voted the NFL's Most Valuable Player by the Associated Press.

Birthdays

9•MUGGSY BOGUES, basketball (1965)

10•GEORGE FOREMAN, boxing (1948)

11•TRACY CAULKINS, swimming (1963)

12•MARK ALLEN, triathlon, (1958)

11 **1987** Denver quarterback John Elway directed one of the greatest drives in NFL playoff history today. He guided the Broncos to a 23–20 win over the Cleveland Browns for the AFC title. Trailing by a touchdown late in the fourth quarter, John marched his team 98 yards in 15 plays to score the tying touchdown with just 37 seconds left. Denver earned a trip to Super Bowl XXI with an overtime field goal.

January 10, 1982: San Francisco receiver Dwight Clark snags an uncatchable pass.

1991 In a meeting of women's college basketball powers, Number 2-ranked Virginia beat Number 3-ranked North Carolina State, 123–120, in triple overtime.

1995 Utah Jazz shooting guard Jeff Hornacek sank his 11th straight 3-point basket, tying the NBA record. (His 11 baskets were spread over six games.)

12 **1969** When New York Jet quarterback Joe Namath guaranteed a victory for his team in Super Bowl III, everybody laughed. The Baltimore Colts were favored to beat New York by two or three touchdowns. But Joe delivered on his promise and led the Jets to a 16–7 Super Bowl win.

1992 It's not often that a basketball team scores 141 points and loses. But that's what happened to DeVry Institute. It lost to Troy State, 258–141!

1994 Pitcher Steve Carlton was voted into baseball's Hall of Fame today. "Lefty" won the Cy Young Award four times as a pitcher for the Philadelphia Phillies. He won 329 games in his career.

1985 Otto Bucher of Switzerland was not only playing golf at the age of 99, he was playing well. While playing in Spain, he got a hole-in-one, becoming the oldest person ever to do so.

1991 Twenty-year-old Phil Mickelson birdied the final hole to win the Northern Telecom Open, in Tucson, Arizona. Phil was the youngest amateur ever to win a PGA Tour event.

1991 The Los Angeles Raiders beat the Cincinnati Bengals, 20–10, in the AFC divisional playoff. Raider running back Bo Jackson suffered a football-career-ending hip injury during the game.

1994 University of California sophomore basketball guard Jason Kidd posted a triple-double today. He scored 17 points, grabbed 11 rebounds, and dished out 11 assists.

1940 Baseball commissioner Kenesaw Mountain Landis made free agents of four Detroit Tiger players and 87 Detroit farm-team players. He did it after ruling that the Tigers had handled players unfairly.

1951 The first NFL Pro Bowl game was held at Los Angeles Memorial Coliseum, in California. The American Conference barely squeaked by the National Conference, 28–27.

1968 Vince Lombardi coached his last game for the Green Bay Packers today. One year after winning Super Bowl I, the Packers beat the Oakland Raiders, 33–14, in Super Bowl II.

1973 The Miami Dolphins completed the only perfect season in NFL history. Miami's 14–7 victory over the Washington Redskins in Super Bowl VII gave the Dolphins a 17–0 record for the season.

Birthdays

13•KENT HULL, football (1961)

14• SONNY SIEBERT, baseball (1937)

15•MARY PIERCE, tennis (1975)

16•A.J. FOYT, auto racing (1935)

15

1892 Rules for a new sport were made public. The new game was called basketball, and was invented by Dr. James Naismith, in Springfield, Massachusetts. The game was played with a soccer ball and a peach basket at each end of the court.

1967 The Green Bay Packers beat the Kansas City Chiefs in the first Super Bowl game. (The first two Super Bowls were called AFL-NFL World Championship Games.)

1984 In a battle of tennis stars from the country of Czechoslovakia, Hana Mandlikova defeated Martina Navratilova to halt Martina's winning streak at 54 matches.

January 13, 1991: Raider Bo Jackson (34) suffers a football-career-ending injury.

16

1970 In a college basketball game at Pacific Lutheran University, Steve Myers made an amazing shot. He did it while standing out of bounds, at the opposite end of his team's court. At first, the 92' 3½" shot was declared illegal. But when the crowd started to boo, officials changed their minds!

1972 The Miami Dolphins became the first team *not* to score a touchdown in the Super Bowl. The Dallas Cowboys won, 24–3.

1994 Kansas City quarterback Joe Montana threw three second-half touchdown passes as the Chiefs rallied from a 10–0 hole to upset the Houston Oilers, 28–20. Kansas City advanced to the AFC title game.

 **1916** The first organizational meeting of the Professional Golfers' Association (PGA) was held today in New York City. (James Barnes of Great Britain will be the winner of the first PGA Championship.)

1971 Together, the Baltimore Colts and Dallas Cowboys commited 11 turnovers in Super Bowl V. The game was so sloppy that many people called it the "Blooper Bowl." The Colts won on a late field goal, 16–13.

1990 Boston Bruin right wing Cam Neely scored three goals, including the game-winner, against the Los Angeles Kings. It was Cam's seventh career *hat trick,* which is the term used when a player scores three goals in one game.

 **1958** Willie O'Ree became the first black player in the NHL when he was called up from the Boston Bruins' farm team. He played in today's game against the Montreal Canadiens. The Bruins beat the Canadiens, 3–0.

1959 Marion Ladewig of Grand Rapids, Michigan, won her seventh All-Star bowling tournament. The greatest woman bowler ever, Marion was voted Woman Bowler of the Year 10 times, a feat that hasn't been matched by any bowler, man or woman.

1976 The Pittsburgh Steelers defeated the Dallas Cowboys, 21–17, to become Super Bowl champions. Pittsburgh receiver Lynn Swann made four spectacular catches for 161 yards. He was named MVP.

1992 The Campbell Conference crushed the Wales Conference, 10–6, in the NHL All-Star Game. (After next season, the NHL will change the conference names to Eastern and Western.) The teams are divided geographically.

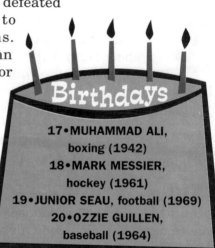

Birthdays

17•MUHAMMAD ALI, boxing (1942)
18•MARK MESSIER, hockey (1961)
19•JUNIOR SEAU, football (1969)
20•OZZIE GUILLEN, baseball (1964)

19

1898 In the first college hockey game, Brown blanked Harvard, 6–0. By the 1940's, college hockey would become as popular as the professional game.

1974 Notre Dame's Dwight Clay sank a jump shot with 29 seconds remaining to give his team a 71–70 upset victory over the UCLA Bruins. The loss snapped the Bruins' 88-game winning streak, the longest in college basketball history. Believe it or not, the Bruins' last loss had come three years earlier on the same court.

1995 With 13 rebounds in Phoenix's 122–115 win at Portland, Charles Barkley passed the 9,000 career-rebound mark.

January 19, 1995: Phoenix Sun forward Charles Barkley passes the 9,000 career-rebound mark.

20

1952 Patricia Mc-Cormick of Big Spring, Texas, became the first woman bullfighter in North America. She killed two of three bulls she faced in a ring in Juarez, Mexico. She dedicated the second bull to her mother. Patricia's success on this day was the start of a long bullfighting career.

1980 Pittsburgh Steeler wide receiver John Stallworth made a Super Bowl-winning catch beyond the outstretched arm of Los Angeles Ram defender Rod Perry. The 73-yard touchdown put the Steelers ahead, 24–19, in the fourth quarter. Minutes later, John made a 45-yard catch, setting up another touchdown. Pittsburgh won its fourth championship in six years, 31–19.

1994 Mike Smith won the Eclipse Award as the best jockey in the country. He rode 353 winners, and the race horses Mike rode earned more than $14 million in purses.

1975 Tonight's NHL All-Star Game made history, but not because of anything that happened on the ice. For the first time in professional sports, female reporters were allowed to enter locker rooms to interview players.

1979 The Pittsburgh Steelers became the first team ever to win three Super Bowls when they defeated the Dallas Cowboys in Super Bowl XIII. Steeler quarterback Terry Bradshaw threw four touchdown passes in the 35–31 victory.

1986 New York Islander Denis Potvin tied an NHL record for defensemen by scoring the 270th goal of his career. He tied Bobby Orr, who had set the record in 1977 when he was playing with the Chicago Blackhawks.

1857 The newly formed National Association of Baseball Players met in New York. The group agreed on some new rules, including a limit of nine innings per game. Until then, games lasted until one team scored 21 runs.

1951 A young Cuban pitcher was thrown out of a winter-league game for hitting a batter with a pitch. The pitcher, whose name was Fidel Castro, decided to give up sports and look for another career. He will become the dictator of Cuba.

1973 Today, George Foreman gave himself a big birthday present: He beat Joe Frazier in the second round to become the world heavyweight champion.

1989 The San Francisco 49ers beat the Cincinnati Bengals in Super Bowl XXIII by the score of 20–16. With a mix of passes and runs, Joe Montana led the team down the field 92 yards in the final minutes and hit John Taylor with a touchdown pass with 34 seconds to go!

Birthdays

21•HAKEEM OLAJUWON, basketball (1963)

22•MIKE BOSSY, hockey (1957)

23•BRENDAN SHANAHAN, hockey (1969)

24•MARY LOU RETTON, gymnastics (1968)

23 **1929** The New York Yankees became the first team to wear permanent numbers on their uniforms. Each player wore a number that was the same as his spot in the batting order. (Babe Ruth batted third and wore number 3.)

1983 At the height of his career, 26-year-old tennis star Bjorn Borg announced his retirement. He had won a record five straight Wimbledon titles.

1992 The financially struggling Seattle Mariners baseball team found a buyer today. The group with the money was led by Hiroshi Yamauchi, president of the Nintendo Company.

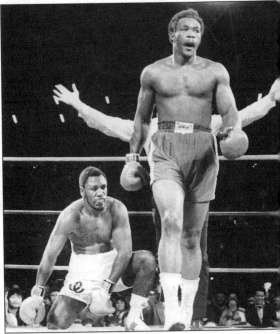

January 22, 1973: George Foreman beats Joe Frazier for the title.

24 **1955** Major league baseball gave new meaning to the word *fastball*. It announced a new rule that required pitchers to deliver the ball within 20 seconds after taking the pitching position. Before that, pitchers could take as long as they wanted. Many fans thought that was just too long!

1959 Walter Stolle of Czechoslovakia set out on what would be the longest bicycle tour in history. Over the course of 17 years, he will visit 159 countries. Walter will have more than 1,000 flat tires along the way.

1981 New York Islander Mike Bossy needed two goals against Quebec to tie Maurice "Rocket" Richard's record of 50 goals in 50 games. With less than five minutes remaining, he finally got one. Then, with 1:29 left on the clock, Mike scored another goal and caught the Rocket.

25

1924 The first Winter Olympics officially opened in Chamonix *[shah-mon-EE]*, France. A total of 294 athletes from 16 countries competed in 14 events. Only 13 competitors were women. They competed in singles and pairs figure skating. Figure skaters performed on the same frozen lake on which hockey and the speed-skating events were held.

1987 Quarterback Phil Simms led the New York Giants to their first football title since 1956. Phil completed 22 of 25 passes to set a Super Bowl record for quarterback accuracy. The Giants beat the Denver Broncos, 39–20. Phil was named MVP.

1989 Michael Jordan of the Chicago Bulls scored the 10,000th point of his career in a 120–108 loss to the Philadelphia 76ers. Mike wasn't the first player to reach the 10,000-point mark, but only Wilt Chamberlain did it in fewer games. Wilt hit 10,000 points in 236 games; Michael did it in 303 games.

26

1960 Pete Rozelle became the National Football League commissioner. At the time, the league had 12 teams. With Pete on the job, the NFL would expand to 28 teams.

1986 The Chicago Bears bombed the New England Patriots, 46–10, in Super Bowl XX. The Bears set eight Super Bowl records and tied 14 others.

1990 Steffi Graf trailed in the second set, but stormed back to defeat Mary Joe Fernandez for her third straight Australian Open title. It was her 48th straight match win.

1997 The Green Bay Packers defeated the New England Patriots, 35–21, in Super Bowl XXXI. It was Green Bay's first championship in 29 years. Punt and kickoff returner Desmond Howard won MVP honors.

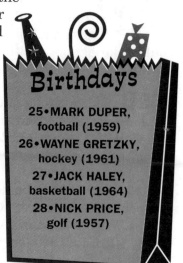

Birthdays

25•MARK DUPER, football (1959)

26•WAYNE GRETZKY, hockey (1961)

27•JACK HALEY, basketball (1964)

28•NICK PRICE, golf (1957)

27 **1984** Wayne Gretzky scored in his 51st straight game, setting an NHL record.

1989 Kenny Anderson, then a high school student in New York City, set a New York State basketball scoring record. Going into today's game, Kenny needed 15 points to break the record of 2,391 points. He did it on a free throw late in the second quarter. The game was stopped while the crowd gave him a standing ovation.

1991 The New York Giants escaped with a narrow 20–19 victory over the Buffalo Bills in Super Bowl XXV. Buffalo placekicker Scott Norwood missed a 47-yard field goal attempt with eight seconds left, preserving the Giants' second Super Bowl victory in five years.

January 25, 1989: Michael Jordan of the Bulls scores his 10,000th career point.

28 **1933** Tennis star Helen Wills Moody scored a big win for women. Helen, who won Wimbledon seven times, defeated Phil Neer in a match. It was the first time a woman beat a man in a professional tennis match.

1943 Chicago Blackhawk forward Max Bentley scored four goals today. Each one came on an assist from his teammate Doug Bentley. Doug was Max's brother!

1995 Utah posted a team record 12th straight win. The Jazz defeated the New Jersey Nets, 111–94, as John Stockton passed Oscar Robertson to take second place on the NBA's all-time assist list, with 9,897.

1936 The first inductees into the Baseball Hall of Fame were announced today. They were Ty Cobb, Babe Ruth, Honus Wagner, Christy Mathewson, and Walter Johnson.

1991 Eric Murdock, a guard for Providence College, broke the NCAA men's basketball record for career steals by snatching number 342 against Seton Hall.

1994 After losing an NBA-record 19 games in a row at home, the Dallas Mavericks finally won a home game. They beat the Sacramento Kings, 108–101.

1993 Monica Seles defeated Steffi Graf to win the Australian Open for the third straight year. The win was Monica's eighth Grand Slam title. Three months later, on April 30, 1993, Monica would be stabbed by a spectator at a tournament in Hamburg, Germany. The attacker was a crazed fan of Steffi's who wanted to get Monica out of Steffi's way.

1994 U.S. speed skater Dan Jansen broke his own 500-meter world record at the World Sprint Speed Skating Championships, in Calgary, Alberta, Canada. Dan finished in 35.76, shaving .16 of a second off his old record.

1994 The Dallas Cowboys won their second straight Super Bowl — while the Buffalo Bills suffered a fourth straight Super Bowl loss. The final score was 30–13. Cowboy running back Emmitt Smith was named the game's MVP.

1996 Magic Johnson ended his 4½-year retirement. In his first game back, he had 19 points, 10 assists, and 8 rebounds, as the Los Angeles Lakers beat the Golden State Warriors, 128–118. Magic retired again after the 1996–97 season.

Birthdays

29•ANDRE REED, football (1964)

30•PAYNE STEWART, golf (1957)

31•JACKIE ROBINSON, baseball (1919)

31•NOLAN RYAN, baseball (1947)

31

1970 Louisiana State University's Pete Maravich became the highest-scoring NCAA Division I basketball player of all time. Pete finished his three-year college career with 3,667 points.

1988 The Washington Redskins exploded for five touchdowns in the second quarter of Super Bowl XXII. Timmy Smith set the Super Bowl record by rushing for 204 yards, as Washington defeated Denver, 42–10.

January 30, 1994: Dan Jansen breaks his own 500-meter world speed-skating record.

1989 In a college basketball game in Los Angeles, California, Loyola Marymount University beat U.S. International University, 181–150, and set two records. Loyola's 181 points were the most ever scored by a college team, and the teams' combined score of 331 points was also the highest ever.

1993 The Dallas Cowboys steamrolled the Buffalo Bills in Super Bowl XXVII, 52–17. Dallas quarterback Troy Aikman, who threw four touchdown passes, was named MVP.

FEBRUARY

February 14, 1992: Bonnie Blair wins her third Olympic gold medal!

1914 A baseball game in the desert? The Chicago White Sox and New York Giants played an exhibition game in front of the Great Pyramids in Egypt. The exhibition was part of a world tour to make baseball more popular. The game ended in a tie.

1970 New York Ranger goalie Terry Sawchuk recorded the 103rd shutout of his career. The Rangers went on to crush the Pittsburgh Penguins, 6–0. Terry was the first player in NHL history to reach 100 shutouts.

1988 Former Chicago Bear Mike Ditka became the first tight end inducted into the Pro Football Hall of Fame. Mike will later coach the Bears, guiding them to 112 wins, six NFC Central titles, and their only Super Bowl victory.

1995 Utah Jazz forward Karl Malone received a crisp bounce pass from teammate John Stockton during the second quarter of a game against the Denver Nuggets. Karl quickly leaped in the air, hitting a corner jump shot. John got the assist, which boosted his career total to 9,922. That moved him past Magic Johnson and into the NBA record books as the all-time leader in assists.

2

1954 Clarence "Bevo" Francis of Rio Grande College, set a college basketball record by scoring an amazing 113 points in a single game.

1991 Jaromir Jagr of the Pittsburgh Penguins got his first NHL hat trick, in a game against the Boston Bruins. Jaromir, who was 18, became the youngest Penguin to score three goals in a game!

1994 Scotty Bowman notched his 1,000th coaching win when his Detroit Red Wings beat the Tampa Bay Lightning. Scotty is the first NHL coach to reach that mark.

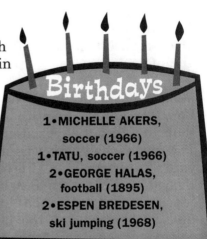

Birthdays

1•MICHELLE AKERS, soccer (1966)

1•TATU, soccer (1966)

2•GEORGE HALAS, football (1895)

2•ESPEN BREDESEN, ski jumping (1968)

3

1956 Flying fruit interrupted the pairs figure skating competition at the Winter Olympics, in Cortina D'Ampezzo, Italy. The audience disagreed with a low score a German pair had received and decided to put the squeeze on the referee and judges by pelting them with oranges.

1990 Bill Shoemaker, the legendary jockey, rode in his final horse race today. "Shoe" is horse racing's all-time leader in wins, with 8,833. Over his amazing career, he won the Preakness twice, the Kentucky Derby four times, and the Belmont five times.

1991 This five-man driving team — John Winter, Frank Jelinski, Henri Pescarolo, Hurley Haywood, and Bob Wollek — won the 24 Hours of Daytona auto race. A team's goal is to cover the most distance in a day. The drivers take turns keeping the car going. The winning team drove more than 2,500 miles in the 24 hours, at an average speed of about 107 miles per hour.

4

1932 The U.S. hosted the Winter Olympics for the first time. Governor Franklin D. Roosevelt of New York welcomed 306 athletes from around the world to Lake Placid, New York. Governor Roosevelt was elected President of the United States in November.

1987 The U.S. thought it had won yachting's America's Cup after Captain Dennis Conner's boat defeated an Australian boat. Unfortunately, the U.S. boat was disqualified because the judges felt it had an unfair design.

1996 The NFC won the Pro Bowl, 20–13. But it was the AFC that provided the excitement! The game's highlight was a 93-yard TD pass from Cincinnati Bengal Jeff Blake to Pittsburgh Steeler Yancey Thigpen in the first quarter. It was the longest scoring play in Pro Bowl history!

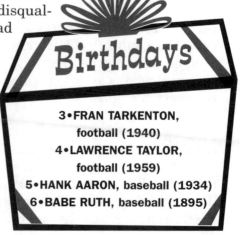

Birthdays

3•FRAN TARKENTON, football (1940)

4•LAWRENCE TAYLOR, football (1959)

5•HANK AARON, baseball (1934)

6•BABE RUTH, baseball (1895)

5

1943 Boxer Jake LaMotta defeated Sugar Ray Robinson today. It was Sugar Ray's first loss in 40 fights. Three weeks later, the two rivals faced off again. But this time Sugar Ray was the winner.

1976 Bill Koch *[coke]* became the first American ever to win an Olympic medal in cross-country skiing. At the Winter Olympics, in Austria, he won a silver medal in the 30-kilometer race. Bill's win helped make cross-country skiing more popular in the U.S.

February 4, 1987: The U.S. crew wins the America's Cup races but is disqualified.

1994 Washington Capital right winger Peter Bondra set the NHL record for the four fastest goals scored. He scored four goals within 4 minutes, 12 seconds!

6

1990 St. Louis Blues right wing Brett Hull notched his 50th goal of the season today. Brett seems to be following in his father's footsteps. His father, Bobby, had scored 50 goals in a season five times during his 23-year career with the Chicago Blackhawks. They became the first father and son in NHL history to each have 50-goal seasons.

1993 Tennis legend Arthur Ashe, who was the first African-American man to win both the United States Open and Wimbledon, died from AIDS-related complications today. Arthur had become as well known for his civil rights work as for his tennis achievements.

1994 Atlanta Falcon wide receiver Andre Rison caught six passes for 86 yards to lead the National Football Conference (NFC) to a 17–3 win over the American Football League Conference (AFC) in the Pro Bowl. The victory was the fourth in six years for the NFC.

7

1969 Diana Crump galloped her way into horse-racing history at Hialeah Race Track, in Florida. She became the first woman jockey to compete in an American thoroughbred horse race.

1976 He shoots, he scores! Toronto Maple Leaf center Darryl Sittler scored 10 points in a game, setting an NHL record. Toronto bombed the Boston Bruins, 11–4.

1985 Marshall University's Bruce Morris was standing 89, feet 10 inches from the basket and time was running out. He was just a few inches from being out-of-bounds at the opposite end of the court. Bruce heaved the ball as far as he could. The shot went up, up, up . . . and in! It was the longest measured basket in a college game.

8

1936 University of Chicago halfback Jay Berwanger became the first player selected in the first NFL draft. He was chosen by the Philadelphia Eagles. In 1935, Jay had been the first player to win the Heisman Trophy, which is given to the nation's top college football player each year.

1981 United States figure skating star Scott Hamilton became the men's U.S. figure skating champion. It was the first of four straight skating titles for Scott.

1986 At 5' 7", Spud Webb is at least six inches shorter than most NBA players. But he rose to new heights to win the NBA's annual slam-dunk contest. Even though he was the smallest player in the competition, Spud out-slammed 1985 champ Dominique Wilkins. Dominique is a whole foot taller than Spud!

1987 Golfing great Nancy Lopez took in another win — this time at the Sarasota Classic. It was her 35th career victory. This LPGA Hall of Famer is a 47-time winner on the LPGA tour.

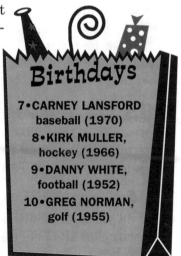

Birthdays

7•CARNEY LANSFORD baseball (1970)

8•KIRK MULLER, hockey (1966)

9•DANNY WHITE, football (1952)

10•GREG NORMAN, golf (1955)

FEBRUARY

1895 Hamline College of St. Paul, Minnesota, defeated the School of Agriculture in the first basketball game between two colleges. The final score was 9–3!

1988 Mario Lemieux of the Pittsburgh Penguins had three goals and three assists to help the Wales Conference win the NHL All-Star Game.

1992 Magic Johnson returned from retirement to play in the NBA All-Star Game. He scored a game-high 25 points, and earned MVP honors as he led the West to a 153–113 victory.

1920 Major League Baseball banned the spitball and all other pitches thrown with a wet or marked-up ball.

1990 James "Buster" Douglas flattened Mike Tyson in the 10th round, to win the heavyweight boxing crown. It was the first loss of Iron Mike's career.

February 8, 1981: Scott Hamilton becomes the men's U.S. figure skating champion.

1992 Speed skater Bonnie Blair won a gold medal in the 500-meters event. That made her the first American woman to win gold medals at back-to-back Olympics.

31

11

1968 It was a basketball free throw bonanza. The University of Cincinnati and Morehead State attempted 111 free throws and made 88, which set an NCAA record for free throws made in a game.

1968 Figure skater Peggy Fleming became the only U.S. athlete to win a gold medal at the 1968 Winter Olympics, in Grenoble, France. She earned every first place vote from the judges.

1973 What a losing streak! The Philadelphia 76ers were hit with their 20th straight loss after getting stomped by the Los Angeles Lakers, 108–90. The Sixers ended the season with a record of 9–73 — the worst ever in NBA history.

1995 Two Miami Heat guards had a hot day at the NBA All-Star Game competitions. Harold Miner won the Slam-Dunk Championship, and Glen Rice won the Long Distance Shootout. It was the first time players from the same team swept those events.

12

1908 The first around-the-world auto race started in New York City. Drivers from the United States, Germany, Italy, and France entered the race. The route went across the United States to Seattle, Washington, by boat to Siberia, in Russia, then through Europe to Paris, France. The American team won, completing the 13,341-mile race in less than six months.

1949 Paul Arizin of Villanova University set an NCAA basketball record by scoring 85 points against the Philadelphia Naval Air Command.

1993 The San Jose Sharks lost their 17th straight game, tying a record set by the Washington Capitals in 1974–75. Two days later, the Sharks ended their streak with a win.

Birthdays

11•MAX BAER, boxing (1909)

12•BILL RUSSELL, basketball (1934)

13•PATTY BERG, golf (1918)

14•JIM KELLY, football (1936)

13 **1954** Frank Selvy of Furman University became the first Division I college basketball player to score 100 points in a game. He scored 100 points in his team's 149–95 win over Newberry. No other Division I player has broken Frank's amazing record!

1988 Jackie Joyner-Kersee set an American indoor long jump record today. She jumped 23' 4¾" at the U.S. Olympic Invitational, at the Meadowlands, in New Jersey.

February 13, 1994: Skier Tommy Moe races to a gold medal in the men's downhill.

1994 Tommy Moe won the gold medal in the men's downhill skiing event to give the U.S. its second-straight Olympic medal.

14 **1953** Bill Chambers of William and Mary College set an NCAA basketball record today. Bill pulled down 51 rebounds in William and Mary's game against the University of Virginia.

1975 The San Diego Conquistadors defeated the New York Nets, 176–166, in the highest scoring game in the history of the American Basketball Association (ABA). The game went to four overtime periods. (The Nets later joined the NBA and moved to New Jersey.)

1992 Speed skater Bonnie Blair won the 1,000-meter event and became the first U.S. woman to win three Winter Olympic gold medals.

1993 NFL head coach Joe Gibbs is a winner in any sport. Joe led the Washington Redskins to three Super Bowl championships. On this day, Joe watched as the stock car he owned won the Daytona 500 with Dale Jarrett behind the wheel.

FEBRUARY

1953 Figure skater Tenley Albright won a spot in the history books by becoming the first American woman to win the world championship in skating. That same year, Tenley took first place at the North American and U.S. championships.

1976 Talk about a wild finish! On the final lap of the Daytona 500 stock-car race, the cars of drivers David Pearson and Richard Petty knocked fenders. Both cars smashed into the wall and spun out — just a few feet from the finish line. David crossed the finish line and won the race. But Richard's car needed a push from his crew to capture second place.

1978 In one of the most amazing upsets in boxing history, Leon Spinks defeated Muhammad Ali for the heavyweight title.

1994 The University of Kentucky pulled off one of the greatest comebacks in college basketball history. After trailing by 31 points in the second half, Kentucky bounced back to defeat Louisiana State University, 99–95.

1987 Cindy Brown of Long Beach State University set an NCAA women's basketball record by scoring 60 points in a game against San Jose State University. Cindy will also set an NCAA record for most points in a season — 974.

1988 King Kong isn't the only one to make a name for himself by climbing New York's Empire State Building. Every year, runners compete to see who can dash up the 86 flights of steps the fastest. This year, Australian Craig Logan won in only 11 minutes, 29 seconds!

1992 Martina Navratilova passed Chris Evert on tennis's all-time list by wining her 158th singles title at the Virginia Slims tournament in Chicago.

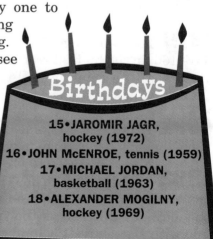

Birthdays

15•JAROMIR JAGR, hockey (1972)

16•JOHN McENROE, tennis (1959)

17•MICHAEL JORDAN, basketball (1963)

18•ALEXANDER MOGILNY, hockey (1969)

FEBRUARY

1955 Golfer Mike Souchak set a PGA record by shooting the Texas Open's back nine in 27 strokes.

1975 Victor Niederhoffer defeated Peter Briggs in three straight sets to win his fifth U.S. squash singles championship. Squash is a fast-paced racket game played in a small room with the ball bouncing off the floor and walls.

1985 Johnny Walker does it again. Today, the New Zealand native ran a mile under four minutes — for the 100th time in his career!

1994 David Robinson of the San Antonio Spurs scored a quadruple double today: 34 points, 10 rebounds, 10 assists, and 10 blocks. It was the fourth quadruple double in history.

February 16, 1992: Tennis great Martina Navratilova clinches her 158th singles title.

1919 Ottawa star Cy Denneny notched the 52nd goal of his career in a 4–3 victory over Toronto. That goal shot Cy to the top of the NHL scoring list.

1979 Auto-racer Richard Petty drove off with his sixth win in the Daytona 500, in Daytona Beach, Florida. Richard is the first race-car driver to win the event six times.

1994 Speed skater Dan Jansen won the Olympic gold medal in the 1,000-meter race in a world record time of 1 minute, 12.43 seconds. Dan had failed to win a medal in three earlier Olympics.

FEBRUARY

19

1928 Fifteen-year-old Sonja Henie of Norway won the gold medal in figure skating. Sonja changed the sport with her jumps and graceful moves. She will win three Olympic gold medals in a row. No other woman has repeated as Olympic singles champion three times.

1984 It was a double win for the Mahre family in the slalom skiing competition at the Winter Olympics, in Sarajevo, Yugoslavia. Twin brothers Steve and Phil Mahre finished in first and second place. Phil took the gold, and Steve won the silver.

1991 Chicago Bull star guard Michael Jordan scored 40 points against the Washington Bullets, giving him at least one 40-point performance against every NBA team (except the NBA's two newest expansion teams).

20

1982 In NHL action, the New York Islanders outskated the Colorado Rockies, 3–2, for their 15th regular-season win in a row. That set an NHL record. The Islanders will go on to win their third of four straight Stanley Cups.

1985 The World Boxing Council (WBC) flyweight champion, Sot Chitalada of Thailand, successfully defended his title against Charlie Magri of Great Britain. But Sot's $97,000 winner's check was stolen by a ringside pickpocket.

1988 It was called the "Battle of the Brians." At the 1988 Winter Olympics, figure skaters Brian Boitano of the U.S. and Brian Orser of Canada battled for the gold medal. In the end, Brian Boitano won.

1994 After 279 Winston Cup races, Sterling Marlin finally won! He beat Ernie Irvan by 0.19 of a second. Sterling had hung in through 18 years and 278 losses on the NASCAR circuit.

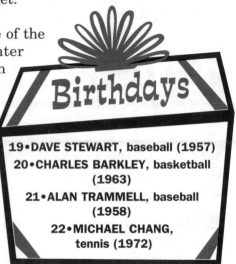

Birthdays

19•DAVE STEWART, baseball (1957)
20•CHARLES BARKLEY, basketball (1963)
21•ALAN TRAMMELL, baseball (1958)
22•MICHAEL CHANG, tennis (1972)

FEBRUARY

21

1980 Hanni Wenzel made the people of Liechtenstein very happy today. The skier took first place in the giant slalom. Hanni became the first person from Liechtenstein (a tiny country in Europe) ever to win an Olympic gold medal.

1992 Kristi Yamaguchi became the first American woman to win an Olympic gold medal in figure skating since Dorothy Hamill, in 1976.

1993 Utah Jazz teammates Karl Malone and John Stockton shared MVP honors at the NBA All-Star Game in

February 22, 1980: The American hockey team performs a "Miracle on Ice."

Salt Lake City, Utah. Cleveland's Mark Price set a record with six 3-point shots in nine attempts. The West won, 135–132.

22

1906 Using a stroke called the "modified Australian crawl," Charles M. Daniels became the first American to swim 100 yards in less than a minute. His time of 57.6 seconds tied the world record.

1980 It's called the "Miracle on Ice," and it was one of the greatest moments in American sports history. The U.S. ice hockey team beat the powerful Soviet Union squad at the Winter Olympics, in Lake Placid, New York. The underdog Americans were trailing, 3–2, when they scored two quick goals for a stunning 4–3 upset. The U.S. went on to win the gold medal against Finland.

1981 What an awesome duo! Brothers Anton and Peter Stastny posted 8 points each to help the Quebec Nordiques defeat the Washington Capitals, 11–7. Their 16 points are a two-man NHL record. Anton and Peter were both NHL rookies at the time.

FEBRUARY

1980 U.S. Olympic speed skater Eric Heiden zoomed into the record books at the Winter Olympics. He became the first athlete to win five gold medals at one Winter Olympics. Eric won five gold medals in nine days.

1987 Nate McMillan of the Seattle SuperSonics proved he was one super Sonic! The rookie guard handed out 25 assists in a game against the Los Angeles Clippers. Nate's one-game total tied the NBA record for most assists by a rookie.

1990 After enjoying a 183-game winning streak in Southwestern Conference play, the University of Texas women's basketball team lost a game. Juliet Jackson of the University of Arkansas sank six free throws down the stretch, for an 82–77 upset.

1994 Way to go, Bonnie! Speed skater Bonnie Blair won her fifth Olympic gold medal, in the 1,000-meter race. She has won more gold medals than any other U.S. woman.

1980 The United States ice hockey team struck down the Finnish team to win the gold medal in the Winter Olympics, in Lake Placid, New York. The victory came two days after the Americans shocked the Soviets and performed their "Miracle on Ice." It was the first gold medal in ice hockey for the United States since 1960.

1982 Wayne Gretzky scored his 77th goal of the season to break Phil Esposito's NHL record. Wayne will end the season with 92 goals and a record 10 hat tricks. (A "hat trick" is three goals in one game.) That's why Wayne is called "The Great One."

1994 At the Winter Olympics, in Lillehammer, Norway, figure skater Oksana Baiul edged out American star Nancy Kerrigan to capture the gold medal in women's singles. Oksana was only 16 years old.

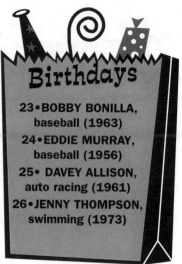

Birthdays

23 • BOBBY BONILLA, baseball (1963)

24 • EDDIE MURRAY, baseball (1956)

25 • DAVEY ALLISON, auto racing (1961)

26 • JENNY THOMPSON, swimming (1973)

25

1964 Cassius Clay shocked Sonny Liston by knocking out the heavyweight champ in Round 7. It was the first heavyweight championship for Cassius, who will later change his name to Muhammad Ali.

1977 "Pistol" Pete Maravich of the New Orleans Jazz (now Utah Jazz) scored 68 points in a game, setting an NBA record for most points ever scored by a guard.

February 24, 1994: Oksana Baiul wows the Olympic audience and wins the gold medal.

1988 Italian ski racer Alberto Tomba's on-the-edge style helped him capture the gold medal in the slalom and giant slalom at the Winter Olympic Games, in Calgary, Alberta, Canada. He won the slalom by .06 of a second. It was the smallest margin of victory at a men's Alpine ski event ever.

26

1935 Could you imagine releasing baseball legend Babe Ruth from the team? That's just what New York Yankee owner Jacob Ruppert did. The Babe was signed by the Boston Braves as a part-time player and assistant manager. On May 25 of the next season, Babe will hit three homers in one game. One week later, he will retire.

1962 Junior middleweight boxer Joseph "Ace" Falu fought his first and only professional fight. He lasted 14 seconds. (Ace was knocked out in the first round.) After the fight, he switched careers.

1995 Anfernee "Penny" Hardaway of the Orlando Magic scored a career-high 39 points, including the game-winning dunk with 0.7 of a second left on the clock. His performance lifted the Magic to a 105–103 victory over the Chicago Bulls.

1980 The Major Indoor Soccer League (MISL) held its first All-Star Game before 16,892 fans in the Checkerdome, in St. Louis, Missouri. The Central Division defeated the Atlantic Division.

1982 Earl Anthony became the first bowler ever to win $1 million in a career. The Hall of Famer from Dublin, California, has won more than 40 Professional Bowlers Association titles.

1988 Katarina Witt of East Germany dazzled the crowd and the judges to win the gold medal in figure skating at the Winter Olympics, in Calgary, Alberta, Canada. She was the first woman since Sonja Henie to win gold medals in back-to-back Olympics.

1992 Sixteen-year-old golfer, Eldrick "Tiger" Woods amazed the golf world when he teed off at the Los Angeles Open. Tiger is the youngest golfer to play in a PGA Tour event.

1960 The U.S. Hockey Team had never won a gold medal in the Winter Olympics. In the championship game, they trailed 4–3 after two periods. But during the final 20 minutes they scored six goals, leading to a 9–4 victory! Roger Christian had four goals. Twenty years later, his son Dave will play on the U.S. Hockey Team that will win the gold medal at the 1980 Winter Olympics.

1981 Calvin Murphy boosted his record streak of consecutive free throws by sinking his 78th in a row. The Houston Rocket had not missed since December 27, 1980.

1985 University of Southern California star Cheryl Miller scored 45 points against the University of Arizona. Cheryl's dominating playing style helped her become USC's all-time leading scorer.

Birthdays

27•JAMES WORTHY, basketball (1961)

28•ERIC LINDROS, hockey (1973)

28•MARIO ANDRETTI, auto racing (1940)

29•CHUCKY BROWN, basketball (1968)

29

1952 Dick Button, the greatest men's figure skater in U.S. history, won his fifth-straight world title. During the year, he also captured the second Olympic gold medal of his six-year career. Dick introduced difficult jumps to men's figure skating. He was the first to perform a triple-loop jump.

1964 It took 13 overtime periods for football teams from Boone Trail and Angier High Schools, in Mamers, North Carolina, to decide the outcome of their game. Boone managed to come out on top, 56–54.

February 28, 1985: USC's Cheryl Miller scores 45 points against Arizona.

1964 Bill McClellon, a New York City high school sophomore, set a national scholastic indoor high-jump record. Bill leaped 6'8" in a local championship meet.

1972 Atlanta Brave slugger Hank Aaron became the highest-paid player in baseball history after signing a three-year contract worth a total of $600,000. Hank will go on to hit more home runs than any other player in major league baseball history.

1980 Gordie Howe became the first NHL player to score 800 goals in a career. Gordie was known as "Mr. Hockey." He played 32 seasons in pro hockey (with the NHL and the World Hockey Association). He retired from the NHL at the end of the 1979–80 season, with 801 goals. He was 51 years old and a grandfather when he hung up the skates.

1992 Boston Bruin defenseman Ray Borque scored the 1,000th point of his NHL career. He is only the third defenseman in NHL history to reach the 1,000-point mark.

MARCH

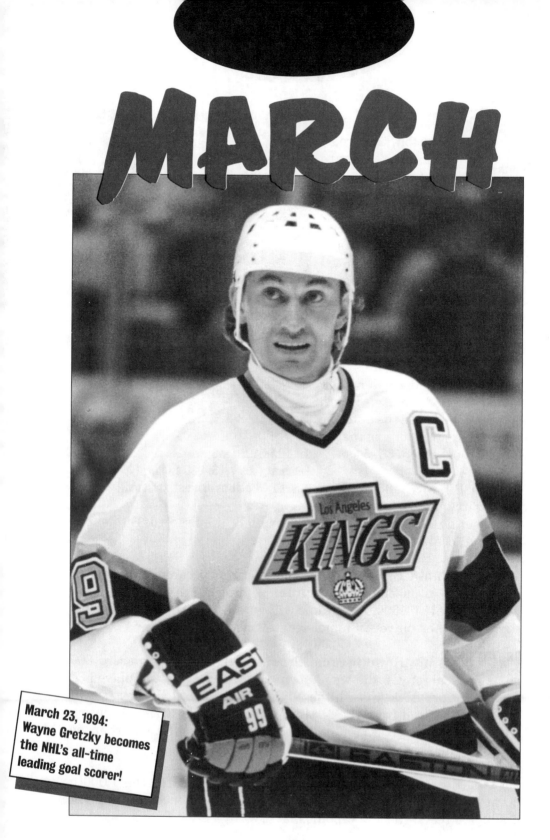

March 23, 1994:
Wayne Gretzky becomes
the NHL's all-time
leading goal scorer!

MARCH

1969 New York Yankee legend Mickey Mantle announced his retirement. Mickey was the greatest switch-hitting slugger in baseball history. He clouted 536 homers in his 18-year career. The centerfielder helped the Yankees reach 12 World Series in his first 14 seasons in the major leagues.

1973 Robyn Smith became the first woman jockey ever to win a major horse-racing stakes race today. Robin rode a horse named North Sea to a first-place finish at Aqueduct, in New York City.

1988 Wayne Gretzky, the Edmonton Oilers' 27-year-old center, notched the 1,050th assist of his career. With it, Wayne jumped ahead of Gordie Howe to become the player with the most assists in NHL history.

1991 Golfer Paul Azinger accidentally moved a pebble with his foot while he was taking his stance at the Doral Ryder Open. That's against the rules in golf. After someone watching the tournament on TV called in to report it, Paul was disqualified!

1951 The first NBA All-Star Game was played today. More than 10,000 fans at the Boston Garden watched the East beat the West, 111–94. "Easy" Ed Macauley of the Boston Celtics led all scorers with 20 points.

1962 Philadelphia Warrior center Wilt Chamberlain put on the most amazing one-man show in NBA history. Playing against the New York Knicks, Wilt scored 100 points in a game, setting an NBA record that may never be broken! Philadelphia won the game, 169–147.

1992 American Anita Nall broke the world 200-meter breast-stroke record today. She did it not once, but *twice,* at the U.S. Olympic Trials!

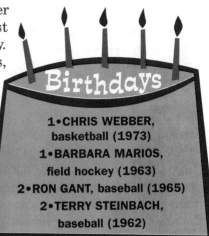

Birthdays

1•CHRIS WEBBER, basketball (1973)

1•BARBARA MARIOS, field hockey (1963)

2•RON GANT, baseball (1965)

2•TERRY STEINBACH, baseball (1962)

3

1975 Francie Larrieu, running for the U.S. in an indoor meet against the Soviet Union, broke two women's world records in the same race. Francie ran the first 1,500 meters of the race in a record 4 minutes, 9.8 seconds and went on to complete a mile in 4 minutes, 28.5 seconds!

1992 The New York Islanders retired Mike Bossy's number 22 jersey today. Mike scored more than 50 goals in a season nine times in a row and helped the Islanders win four straight Stanley Cups.

1995 NBA forward A.C. Green played in his 707th straight game. The streak put A.C. in the Number 3 spot on the all-time consecutive-games-played list. On November 20, 1997, A.C. would become basketball's Iron Man by playing in his 907th game in a row.

4

1941 Chicago Blackhawk goaltender Sam LoPresti stopped an NHL-record 80 shots against the Boston Bruins. Too bad he missed three shots — Chicago ended up losing the game, 3–2.

1973 Chris Evert won her first professional tennis match today. Chris beat Great Britain's Virginia Wade in an S&H Green Stamps event in Florida. Starting in 1974, Chris will win at least one Grand Slam title every year until 1986.

1992 Dennis Rodman of the Detroit Pistons grabbed 34 rebounds in a game against the Indiana Pacers. Dennis was the NBA's top rebounder in 1991–92. He averaged 18.7 rebounds per game.

1996 During the 1990's, linebacker Cornelius Bennett helped the Buffalo Bills win four AFC titles. Today, Cornelius became an Atlanta Falcon! He signed a four-year, $13.6-million contract, which made him the highest-paid player in Atlanta's history.

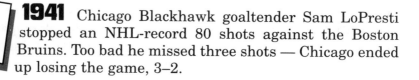

Birthdays

3•JACKIE JOYNER-KERSEE, track and field (1962)
4•KEVIN JOHNSON, basketball (1966)
5•MICHAEL IRVIN, football (1966)
6•SHAQUILLE O'NEAL, basketball (1972)

5

1924 Frank Carauna of Buffalo, New York, bowled a perfect game. Then he bowled another perfect game. After five more strikes, he finally missed a pin. In all, Frank rolled 29 strikes in a row!

1983 Cris Collinsworth, a wide receiver with the Cincinnati Bengals, challenged a horse named "Mr. Hurry" to a race today. Mr. Hurry hurried through the 40-yard race. He easily beat Mr. Collinsworth.

March 6, 1988: Julie Krone becomes the winningest woman jockey of all time!

1994 American sprinter Gwen Torrence won the 200-meter dash at the USA/Mobil Indoor Track and Field Championships. Gwen's time — 22.74 seconds — set a U.S. indoor record.

6

1976 Dorothy Hamill won the world figure skating title and earned a skating triple crown. (She won both an Olympic gold medal and the national title in the same year.) Dorothy, who was a popular champion, also invented her own spin. It's called the Hamill camel.

1988 Julie Krone rode Squawter to victory and headed to the winner's circle for the 1,205th time in her horse-racing career. Since winning her first race, in 1981, Julie has won more races than any other woman jockey.

1990 In her first professional tennis match, 13-year-old Jennifer Capriati knocked off 28-year-old Mary Lou Daniels in straight sets at the Virginia Slims of Boca Raton, Florida. Though she lost to Gabriela Sabatini, Jennifer became the youngest player ever to reach a tournament final.

7

1970 Austin Carr of the University of Notre Dame exploded for 61 points to set a single-game scoring record for the NCAA basketball tournament. Austin led the Fighting Irish to a first-round win over Ohio University.

1983 Phil Mahre became only the third person in history to win the World Cup overall championship in Alpine skiing three straight years. In 1981 he had become the first American skier to win the World Cup title.

1989 Tom Jordan was on a roll. The bowler from Paterson, New Jersey, rolled the best three-game series recognized by the American Bowling Congress in regular-league play. The only pin Tom missed in his near-perfect 899 series was the 10 pin in the last frame of his second game.

8

1971 It was "The Fight of the Century." The match, at New York City's Madison Square Garden, pitted Muhammad Ali against Joe Frazier. Muhammad had been heavyweight champion, but his title was taken away after he refused to be drafted into military service. Smokin' Joe was now the champ. Joe kept his title with a 15-round decision. It was Muhammad's first loss in 32 pro fights.

1992 Bill Elliot won the Pontiac 400 auto race, in Richmond, Virginia. He got a $272,700 first prize and a bonus of $197,600. (The bonus came from a company that had donated money.) To get the bonus, Bill had to qualify for pole position *and* win the race. He did both!

1993 Speed skater Bonnie Blair received the Sullivan Award today. The Amateur Athletic Union gives out the award every year. It goes to the athlete who "by his or her performance, example, and influence as an amateur, has done the most during the year to advance the cause of sportsmanship."

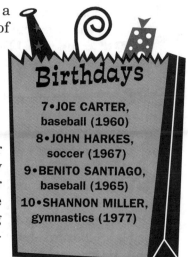

Birthdays

7 • JOE CARTER, baseball (1960)

8 • JOHN HARKES, soccer (1967)

9 • BENITO SANTIAGO, baseball (1965)

10 • SHANNON MILLER, gymnastics (1977)

9

1897 Baseball's Cleveland Spiders signed Louis Sockalexis today. Louis was a Penobscot Native American Indian. The Spiders had a terrible year, but Louis had a great one. He batted .338! Cleveland fans called their team the Indians because of Louis. In 1915, the Spiders were officially renamed the Indians.

1994 Mike Gartner of the New York Rangers scored his 611th goal. He moved into fifth place on the NHL career scoring list.

1995 The San Antonio Spurs stunned the Cleveland Cavaliers with a last-second, 100–98 win. Sean Elliott took a half-court pass from Doc Rivers and sank the ball at the buzzer.

March 7, 1983: Phil Mahre *(left)* wins his third straight World Cup overall title.

10

1896 The first marathon of the modern age was run in Athens, Greece, today. It was a trial run for the marathon at the first modern Olympics. The first-ever marathon was run in 490 B.C. A messenger ran 26 miles to say that the Greeks had won the Battle of Marathon. After he delivered the good news, the messenger dropped dead.

1990 Jill Trenary of the United States won the world figure skating title today. She beat Japan's Midori Ito with a first-place finish in the compulsory figures.

1993 Canada's Isabelle Brasseur and Lloyd Eisler won the pairs title at the World Figure Skating Championships. They broke a nine-year reign by pairs from the former Soviet Union.

11

1945 Byron Nelson won the Miami (Florida) Four Ball tournament and began the greatest hot streak in golfing history. After Miami, Byron finished in first place in his next 10 tournaments.

1992 Most races are timed with a stopwatch. But the most famous sled-dog race is timed with a calendar. The race takes *days* to finish! Martin Buser won this year's Iditarod Trail Sled Dog Race in 10 days, 19 hours, 17 minutes, 15 seconds. The race covers more than 1,100 miles of mountain ranges, forests, and frozen rivers in Alaska. No wonder the goal for most drivers is just to finish!

1993 Canada's Kurt Browning won the world figure skating title at the championships, in Prague, Czechoslovakia. Kurt had finished sixth in the previous year's Olympics. He came back strong to win the world title for the fourth time in five years.

12

1966 He was so fast, he was known as the Golden Jet. Chicago Blackhawk Bobby Hull was one of the best left wings in the history of hockey. His slap shot was once clocked at 118 miles per hour! Today, Bobby became the first NHL player to score more than 50 goals in a season when he scored his 51st goal in this season's 61st game. He will increase his record to 54 goals by the end of the season.

1991 Retired Hall of Fame pitcher Jim Palmer ended his comeback bid with the Baltimore Orioles. Jim had retired after the 1984 season.

1993 Gail Devers of the United States won the 60-meter dash at the World Indoor Track and Field Championships, in Toronto, Canada. She beat world record-holder Irina Privalova of Russia. Gail, whose time was 6.95 seconds, set an American record. In 1992, Gail had won an Olympic gold medal in the 100-meter event.

Birthdays

11•LOUISE BROUGH-CLAPP, tennis (1923)
12•ISAIAH RIDER, basketball (1971)
13•WILL CLARK, baseball (1964)
14•KIRBY PUCKETT, baseball (1961)

13 **1961** American Floyd Patterson defended his heavyweight title against Swedish boxer Ingemar Johansson today. Floyd survived two first-round knockdowns. He won the bout with a sixth-round knockout.

1981 Kevin Slaten of the St. Louis Steamers was thrown out of a Major Indoor Soccer League playoff game for trying to punch a player from the other team. But Kevin wasn't a player for the Steamers — he was the team's announcer!

March 12, 1993: Olympic champion Gail Devers sets a U.S. track-and-field record.

1993 Oksana Baiul won the world figure skating title today. She became the youngest women's champ ever. Oksana, who is from Ukraine, was 15 when she captured the title.

14 **1936** Tennis players Alex Ehrlich of Poland and Farcas Paneth of Romania had the longest volley in the history of the sport. It took them two hours and five minutes to score the first point in a match.

1990 Susan Butcher won the Iditarod sled dog race for the fourth time in five years. Women have won the grueling competition five times between 1985 and 1990. Libby Riddles became the first woman to win the race, in 1985, and Susan won in 1986, 1987, 1988, and 1990.

1993 Butch Reynolds of the United States made a couple of trips to the winner's platform at the World Indoor Track and Field Championships, in Toronto, Canada. Butch won the 400 meters in 45.26 seconds, and he anchored the winning 4x400 relay team.

15

1869 The first baseball team completely made up of professional players was the Cincinnati Red Stockings. Today, the Red Stockings played their first game. They beat Antioch, 41–7. They finished their first season without a defeat, winning 56 games and tying once.

1970 Bobby Orr of the Boston Bruins became the first defenseman in NHL history to score 100 points in a season. Bobby scored two goals and assisted on two others in a game against the Detroit Red Wings, bringing his point total to 101.

1990 In an NCAA swim meet, Janet Evans of Stanford University won the 500-yard freestyle race and set a new U.S. record. Janet, who had won three gold medals at the 1988 Olympics, would win one more at the 1992 Games.

16

1938 College basketball held its first national championship game, in New York City. It was called the National Invitational Tournament (NIT). Temple University beat Colorado, 60–36, to win the title. These days, the NCAA tournament decides college basketball's national champion.

1947 Detroit's Billy Taylor set an NHL record by collecting seven assists today. The record would stand for almost 33 years before being tied by Wayne Gretzky (of course!).

1991 American figure skaters Kristi Yamaguchi, Tonya Harding, and Nancy Kerrigan made skating history when they finished 1–2–3 at the world championships. It was the first time that one country had swept all three medals at the worlds.

1991 At an indoor meet in Spain, pole vaulter Sergei Bubka became the first person ever to vault 20 feet. He cleared 20' ¼" on his first attempt.

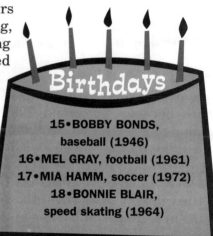

Birthdays

15•BOBBY BONDS, baseball (1946)
16•MEL GRAY, football (1961)
17•MIA HAMM, soccer (1972)
18•BONNIE BLAIR, speed skating (1964)

17 **1876** Marshall Jones Brooks became the first man to jump higher than six feet — just barely — in the high jump. Marshall's jump of 6' ⅛" at a meet in England set a world record. (The world record in the outdoor high jump is now just over eight feet!)

March 16, 1991: **Kristi Yamaguchi wins the figure-skating world championship.**

1984 Swimmer Tracy Caulkins set four meet records today. She also helped the University of Florida win two record-setting relay races at the NCAA women's swimming and diving championships.

1990 In a junior welterweight title bout, Julio Cesar Chavez beat Meldrick Taylor. Julio pounded Meldrick in the 12th and final round. The ref stopped the fight with two seconds left on the clock.

18 **1945** Maurice "Rocket" Richard of the Montreal Canadiens became the first player to score 50 goals in an NHL season. Rocket will go on to score 544 goals over the course of his career and play on eight Stanley Cup championship teams.

1983 Michael Spinks, the World Boxing Association (WBA) champion, outpointed Dwight Braxton, the World Boxing Council (WBC) champion, to unify the light heavyweight championship.

1994 Dallas Star goaltender Andy Moog successfully defended his net in a 6–2 win over the Washington Capitals. It was Andy's 300th career victory. By season's end, he will raise his lifetime total to 313. He is ranked eighth on the all-time win list.

19

1953 Bob Lochmueller of the Syracuse Nationals basketball team set a foul record today. He fouled out of a playoff game against the Boston Celtics after just seven minutes of play, faster than anyone has ever fouled out of an NBA game. (The Nationals later became the Philadelphia 76ers.)

1994 Pat Smith of Oklahoma State University became the first four-time NCAA Division I wrestling champion. He outpointed Sean Bormet of Michigan, 5–3, in the 158-pound division.

1995 Michael Jordan played in his first NBA game since coming out of retirement. Michael scored 19 points, but the Indiana Pacers defeated his Chicago Bulls, 103–96. It was Mike's first game since June 20, 1993.

20

1965 Bill Bradley scored 58 points in the last game of his college basketball career. He led Princeton University to a 118–82 rout over Wichita State in the Final Four consolation game at the NCAA tournament. (The consolation game is no longer played.) Bill's game total was an NCAA record. His tournament total of 177 was also a record. After college, Bill went on to play 10 seasons with the New York Knicks, winning two NBA titles. (Bill later became a U.S. senator from New Jersey.)

1992 Kenny Bernstein became the first drag racer ever to break 300 miles per hour (301.7 m.p.h.). He did it in a qualifying run at the NHRA's Gatornationals, in Gainesville, Florida. Workers at the end of the track held up three fingers — a signal that the 300-m.p.h. barrier had been broken.

1993 The University of Iowa Hawkeyes won their third straight NCAA wrestling championship. It is the team's 12th national title under coach Dan Gable.

Birthdays

19•IVAN CALDERON, baseball (1962)
20•PAT RILEY, basketball (1945)
21•AL IAFRATE, hockey (1966)
22•SHAWN BRADLEY, basketball (1972)

MARCH

21 **1934** Babe Didriksen became the first woman to pitch in a major league baseball game. She pitched for the Philadelphia Athletics in an exhibition game against the Brooklyn Dodgers. The third batter she faced hit into a triple play.

1946 A year *before* Jackie Robinson broke major league baseball's color barrier, Kenny Washington became the first black athlete ever to join an NFL team. On this day, Kenny signed with the Los Angeles Rams.

March 19, 1995: Michael Jordan bounces back into professional basketball.

1992 Runner Lynn Jennings of the United States won her third straight World Cross Country Championship.

22 **1893** Smith College became the first women's school to play basketball. Since there were no other college teams to play against, the Smith students played each other! As part of their uniforms, the players wore bloomers (loose-fitting pants). The women's uniforms were considered so shocking that men were not allowed to watch them play.

1973 A great tennis rivalry began today — Chris Evert and Martina Navratilova played each other for the first time, in a match in Akron, Ohio. Chris won the match in straight sets. Over the next 15 years, the two will face off 80 times. Martina will hold a slim advantage, winning 43 of their matches.

1994 The NFL underwent its first scoring change in 75 years today. Team owners voted to include a 2-point conversion rule after touchdowns.

23

1952 If you blinked, you might have missed it. Bill Mosienko of the Chicago Blackhawks scored the fastest hat trick in NHL history today. He netted three goals in the third period of a game against the New York Rangers in a span of just 21 seconds! Chicago outscored New York, 7–6.

1957 The University of North Carolina Tar Heels and Kansas University Jayhawks played the longest NCAA championship basketball game in history. Kansas, with Wilt Chamberlain, led Carolina by 1 point with six seconds left in triple overtime. But Tar Heel Joe Quigg hit two free throws to give Carolina a 54–53 victory.

1994 Los Angeles King Wayne Gretzky became the NHL's all-time leading goal scorer today. Wayne sent the puck past Vancouver Canuck goalie Kirk McLean for his 802nd career goal. That was one more than the 801 scored by his boyhood idol, Gordie Howe.

24

1936 The longest battle in NHL history was fought today. The game, between the Detroit Red Wings and Montreal Maroons, went on for six overtime periods. It totaled 2 hours, 56 minutes, 30 seconds of playing time. (That's about three times longer than a standard game.) Six hours after it began, the game ended. It was almost 2:30 in the morning!

1980 The University of Louisville shocked the University of California at Los Angeles (UCLA), 59–54, to ruin UCLA's hopes for an 11th national basketball title. It was the first national basketball championship for Louisville. In 1995, the Bruins will win that 11th title.

1995 Seattle SuperSonic Gary Payton made 15 of 17 field goal attempts and scored 32 points today. He helped the SuperSonics nip the Portland Trail Blazers, 122–118. Gary averaged 20.6 points, 7.1 assists, and 2.49 steals per game for the season. He was selected to the All-NBA second team.

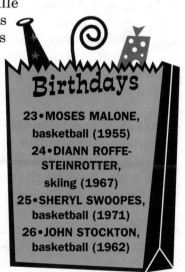

Birthdays

23 • MOSES MALONE, basketball (1955)

24 • DIANN ROFFE-STEINROTTER, skiing (1967)

25 • SHERYL SWOOPES, basketball (1971)

26 • JOHN STOCKTON, basketball (1962)

25 **1982** Wayne Gretzky of the Edmonton Oilers became the first NHL player to score more than 200 points in a season. Wayne scored twice and had two assists in today's win over the Calgary Flames. He will finish the year with 212 points — 48 points more than his old record.

1990 Robert Gamez, a PGA rookie, hit a 7-iron 176 yards into the 72nd and final hole of the Nestlé Invitational for an eagle two. He won the tournament by one stroke.

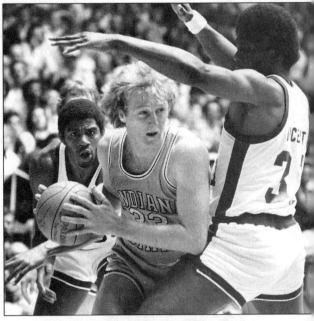

March 26, 1979: Magic Johnson *(left)* and Larry Bird faced off in the NCAA final.

1995 Dana Barros of the Philadelphia 76ers hit a 3-point field goal with 7.9 seconds left in his team's loss to the Indiana Pacers. It was the 44th straight game in which he had made a 3-pointer — an NBA record!

26 **1973** UCLA center Bill Walton made 21 of 22 shots today. His 44 points led the Bruins to their seventh straight NCAA championship and their 75th win in a row. UCLA defeated Memphis State, 87–66.

1979 Basketball's long-running Larry and Magic show debuted in the NCAA tournament finals as Magic Johnson's Michigan State team met Larry Bird's Indiana State team. Michigan won, 75–64, as Magic scored 24 points and was named the tournament's Most Outstanding Player.

1994 John Stockton recorded his 2,000th career steal in a game against Houston today. The Utah Jazz point guard became the second player ever to reach that mark. John finished the season with 2,225 steals, just 85 behind the leader, Maurice Cheeks.

27 **1939** The first NCAA basketball championship game was held at Northwestern University, outside Chicago, Illinois. A crowd of 5,000 fans watched the University of Oregon Tall Firs defeat the Ohio State Buckeyes, 46–33.

1978 Jack "Goose" Givens scored 41 points to lead the University of Kentucky to its first NCAA basketball title in 20 years. Jack, a 6' 4" forward, connected on 18 of 27 field goal attempts. The Wildcats defeated Duke University to cap a 30–2 season with the fifth NCAA basketball title in their history.

1994 Golfer Greg Norman shot 25 birdies to win the Tour Players Championship by four strokes with a course-record 24-under-par 264. "The Shark," as Greg is known, shot over par on just one of the tournament's 72 holes!

28 **1982** The final game of the first NCAA women's basketball tournament was played today. Louisiana Technical University beat Cheyney State University of Pennsylvania, 76–62. Before this, the only national championship for women was held by the Association for Intercollegiate Athletics for Women.

1984 Bye-bye, Baltimore! Colts owner Robert Irsay ordered a fleet of moving vans to be loaded up with the Baltimore Colts' equipment. They were leaving town and moving to Indianapolis. The Baltimore team was one of pro football's most successful franchises.

1995 Just nine days after his return from basketball retirement, Michael Jordan scored 55 points to lead the Chicago Bulls to a 113–111 win over the New York Knicks. Michael was back!

Birthdays

27•RANDALL CUNNINGHAM, football (1963)
28•BYRON SCOTT, basketball (1961)
29•CY YOUNG, baseball (1867)
30•CHRISTOPHER BOWMAN, figure skating

29

1976 In 1975, the Indiana University basketball team had taken a perfect record into the NCAA tournament — and lost. This season, Indiana was undefeated again. This time Indiana beat the University of Michigan, 86–68, to win the title and complete a perfect season!

1982 Michael Jordan scored the basket that won the NCAA championship for the University of North Carolina. The freshman guard scored with 15 seconds left and North Carolina beat Georgetown 63–62.

March 29, 1990: Hakeem Olajuwon records the third quadruple-double in NBA history!

1990 Houston Rocket center Hakeem Olajuwon recorded the third quadruple-double in NBA history. In a game against the Milwaukee Bucks, Hakeem had 18 points, 16 rebounds, 11 blocked shots, and 10 assists.

30

1987 A huge number of fans — 64,959 — came out to the Superdome, in New Orleans, Louisiana, to watch the NCAA men's basketball finals. They saw Indiana University edge Syracuse University, 74–73. The attendance figure was an NCAA college basketball finals record.

1993 The Ottawa Senators tied an 18-year-old NHL record when they lost their 37th straight road game. The Pittsburgh Penguins handed the Senators a 6–4 loss. Ottawa would end the season with a 10–70–4 record.

1994 Janet Evans captured her 37th national swimming title, winning the 800-meter freestyle at the U.S. championships. The victory moved Janet ahead of Johnny Weismuller into second place on the all-time national titles list.

1923 The first dance marathon began at the Audubon Ballroom, in New York City. It lasted 27 hours! Alma Cummings was the only one left dancing as the marathon came to an end.

1931 Knute Rockne, the head football coach at the University of Notre Dame, was killed when the plane he was on crashed in Kansas. During his 13 years as coach, the Fighting Irish won three national championships and finished a season undefeated five times. His career winning percentage of .881 is the best in college football history. Knute was known for his halftime pep talks, including the famous "Win one for the Gipper!" speech.

1985 The first Wrestlemania was held before 23,000 screaming fans in New York City's Madison Square Garden. In a tag-team match, Hulk Hogan and Mr. T defeated "Rowdy" Roddy Piper and Paul Orndoff. Boxing legend Muhammad Ali was the referee.

1994 The Chicago White Sox assigned Michael Jordan to the Birmingham Barons of the Class AA Southern League. For the season, Michael will bat .202, with three home runs, 51 RBIs, and 30 stolen bases. Not bad for a guy who hadn't played baseball since high school!

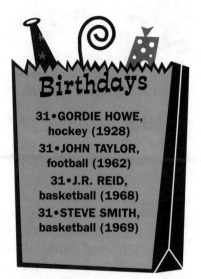

Birthdays

31•GORDIE HOWE,
hockey (1928)
31•JOHN TAYLOR,
football (1962)
31•J.R. REID,
basketball (1968)
31•STEVE SMITH,
basketball (1969)

APRIL

April 15, 1947:
Jackie Robinson
breaks into major
league baseball.

1972 "Strike!" That wasn't an umpire's call. It was a strike called by the players. Major league baseball's first player strike started today. The walkout lasted until April 13, and the season began two days later.

1985 In one of the biggest upsets in NCAA championship history, Villanova nipped Georgetown, 66–64. The Wildcats hit 79 percent of their shots from the field against the Hoyas' top-ranked defense.

1989 David Wharton dove into the national collegiate men's swimming championships in Indianapolis, Indiana. David, who has severe hearing loss, was a big winner today. He took the 200-yard and 400-yard individual medley titles.

1931 Jackie Mitchell became the first woman to pitch on a men's professional baseball team. The 17-year-old signed a minor league contract with the Chattanooga Baseball Club of the Southern Association. She was the starting pitcher in today's exhibition game. Jackie fanned two batters in a row — Babe Ruth and Lou Gehrig!

1990 Today's NCAA final game was the most lopsided basketball final in history. The Runnin' Rebels of the University of Nevada at Las Vegas (UNLV) crushed Duke University, 103–73.

1991 It was Ryan against Ryan when the Texas Rangers took on the University of Texas Longhorns today. Longhorn pitcher Reid Ryan gave up four runs in two innings. Reid's father, Nolan Ryan, started for Texas. He gave up three runs over five innings. Dad got credit for the Rangers' 12–5 victory.

1993 Mark Price of the Cleveland Cavaliers finally missed a free throw, after sinking 77 in a row. Mark had not missed since February 5!

Birthdays

1•MARK JACKSON,
basketball (1965)

2•LINFORD CHRISTIE,
track and field (1960)

3•RODNEY HAMPTON,
football (1969)

4•JULI FURTADO,
mountain biking (1967)

3 **1994** Arnie Boldt of Canada has just one leg, but he didn't let that hold him back today. Arnie soared through the air, clearing 6' 8¼" in the high-jump event at a track-and-field meet in Rome, Italy.

1994 Charlotte Smith sank a 3-point shot at the buzzer in the NCAA women's basketball championship game. The shot gave the University of North Carolina a 60–59 win over Louisiana Tech and its first NCAA women's basketball title.

April 4, 1993: Sheryl Swoopes scores 47 points to lift Texas Tech to the NCAA championship!

1994 For the first time in baseball history, an opening-day game was played at night. The St. Louis Cardinals took on the Cincinnati Reds under the stars and beat them, 6–4.

4 **1974** About 52,000 fans packed Riverfront Stadium to watch the Cincinnati Reds take on the Atlanta Braves. They weren't there just to see the game — they wanted to see Atlanta's Hank Aaron try to tie Babe Ruth's record of 714 career home runs. Hank smacked a homer in his first at-bat! Four days later, "Hammerin' Hank" *broke* the Babe's record.

1988 George Bell of the Toronto Blue Jays became the first player ever to hit three homers on an opening day. George led the Blue Jays to a 5–3 victory over the Kansas City Royals.

1993 Sheryl Swoopes scored 47 points in the NCAA women's basketball final today. She powered Texas Tech to an 84–82 win over Ohio State. Sheryl's 47 points broke the record for most points scored by one player in an NCAA championship game, women's or men's.

61

5

1984 Near the end of the Los Angeles Laker win over Utah, Kareem Abdul-Jabbar sank a very big skyhook — the two points gave him 31,421 for his career. Those two points made him the NBA's all-time leading scorer. (By the time Kareem retired, in 1988, he had raised his career total to 38,387 points.)

1987 In a thrilling duel, golfer Betsy King won the Nabisco Dinah Shore over Patty Sheehan. It was her first major title.

1993 Play ball! Baseball's newest teams, the Florida Marlins and the Colorado Rockies, made their debuts. The Marlins won their first game, but the Rockies lost in a shutout.

6

1893 Boxers Andy Bowen and Jack Burke gave fans their money's worth today. They fought for 110 rounds! The longest bout in history was declared a draw. (After 110 rounds, the boxers were just too pooped to punch.)

1973 In the first inning on opening day, Ron Blomberg stepped into the batter's box and made history. The New York Yankee was the first designated hitter to bat in a major league game. Ron walked with the bases loaded! (Because it was a walk, the first plate appearance by a DH was not an official at-bat.)

1975 Dave Shultz of the Philadelphia Flyers spent seven minutes in the penalty box today, bringing his season total to 472. That's 7 hours and 52 minutes! Dave set a new record for the most penalty minutes in one season.

1987 Sugar Ray Leonard, who had not fought for three years, returned to the ring. There he faced middleweight champ "Marvelous" Marvin Hagler. Sugar Ray won the bout in a decision.

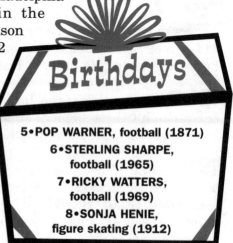

Birthdays

5•POP WARNER, football (1871)

6•STERLING SHARPE, football (1965)

7•RICKY WATTERS, football (1969)

8•SONJA HENIE, figure skating (1912)

7 **1943** The NFL decided that all players had to wear helmets. The first helmets were very thin, made of leather, and had no face mask.

1979 Houston Astro pitcher Ken Forsch hurled a no-hitter to beat the Atlanta Braves today. Bob Forsch (Ken's brother) had pitched his own no-hitter in 1978. The Forsches became the only brothers to pitch no-hitters in the major leagues.

April 8, 1974: Hank Aaron hits his 715th homer, breaking Babe Ruth's record.

1989 Point guard John Stockton of the Utah Jazz passed for his 1,000th assist of the season today. It was the second season in a row that John had made more than 1,000 assists. He was the first player in NBA history to do so.

8 **1974** Atlanta Brave slugger Henry Aaron smacked his 715th home run — one more than Babe Ruth had hit in his career. The homer gave "Hammerin' Hank" the top spot on the career home run list. (By the time he retires, Hank will have hit 755 home runs.)

1975 Twenty-eight years after Jackie Robinson broke baseball's color barrier as a player, Frank Robinson became the game's first black manager. Frank, who was a player-manager, slugged a home run in the first inning of his first game.

1993 Carlos Baerga became the first player to hit home runs from both sides of the plate in the same inning. Batting right-handed, the Cleveland Indian hit a homer off Yankee Steve Howe. His second homer of the inning came as a lefty against Steve Farr.

APRIL

1965 The world's first domed stadium opened in Houston. More than 47,000 fans were in the seats for the first event in the Astrodome. They watched the Astros play the New York Yankees in an exhibition game.

1978 The NBA scoring race came down to the final game. David Thompson of Denver and George Gervin of San Antonio were neck and neck. David scored 73 points in his game to finish with a 27.15 average. George needed 59 points to beat him. He scored 63! George finished with a 27.2 average and the scoring title!

1993 The Pittsburgh Penguins won their 16th game in a row. The record-setting win came against the New York Rangers. The next night, the Penguins beat the Rangers again, stretching the streak to 17.

1993 Bo Jackson had spent a year and a half recovering from hip replacement surgery. Today, he stepped up to the plate for the first time in 18 months and slammed a pinch-hit home run!

1993 The Ottawa Senators snapped their record-setting 38-game losing streak today. Laurie Boschman scored two late goals to lift the Senators over the New York Islanders, 5–3, at Nassau Coliseum.

1993 Bowler Del Ballard won the United States Open, 237–193. (Del came back strong after an embarrassing moment in 1991. In a televised final, he needed a seven in the 10th frame to win the Fair Lanes Open. Instead, he threw a gutter ball!)

1994 Jose Maria Olazabal (*oh-luh-THAH-bull*) of Spain putted well enough to earn first prize in the Masters. Jose beat American Tom Lehman by two strokes. He became the sixth European golfer to win the Masters in the last seven years.

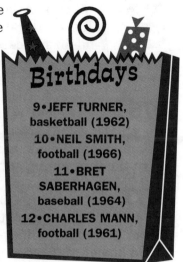

Birthdays

9•JEFF TURNER, basketball (1962)

10•NEIL SMITH, football (1966)

11•BRET SABERHAGEN, baseball (1964)

12•CHARLES MANN, football (1961)

11

1962 A baseball team called the New York Metropolitans (known as the Mets) played their first game today. They also suffered their first loss. And that was just the beginning. The Mets will lose a record 120 games in the season!

1989 Philadelphia Flyer Ron Hextall became the first goalie in Stanley Cup playoff history to score a goal. He shot the puck into an empty net in Game 5 of the Division semi-finals.

April 11, 1989: Ron Hextall becomes the first goalie ever to score a playoff goal.

1995 Jason Kidd posted a remarkable triple-double. The Dallas rookie scored a career-high 38 points to go along with 11 rebounds and 10 assists. For Jason, it was his third triple-double in five games. The Mavericks outgunned Houston, 156–147, in a wild double-overtime game.

12

1958 Last year, the Boston Celtics beat the St. Louis Hawks in the NBA Finals. This year, St. Louis took its revenge. The Hawks defeated the Celtics 110–109 and became champions of the NBA. St. Louis forward Bob Pettit scored 50 points!

1987 At the Masters golf tournament, Greg Norman and Larry Mize were tied at the end of regulation play. The first player to win a hole in the sudden-death playoff would win the tournament. Larry sank an amazing 140-foot chip shot to win it all.

1994 Scott Cooper of the Boston Red Sox hit for the cycle. He smacked a single, double, triple, and homer in today's game against Kansas City. Scott was the first player to hit for the cycle since 1991.

13

1978 It rained candy bars at Yankee Stadium today. The 45,000 fans received Reggie Jackson candy bars when they arrived. After Reggie homered in his first at-bat, thousands of Reggie bars were thrown onto the field.

1984 On this day in 1963, Pete Rose got his first major league hit. Today, Pete celebrated by getting a double off Philadelphia pitcher Jerry Koosman. It was Pete's 4,000th career hit!

1997 Tiger Woods, age 21, became the youngest man ever to win the Masters. He also became the first black golfer to win a major tournament. Tiger's 18-under-par score of 270 was the lowest in the history of the Masters. He won by 12 strokes. It was the largest margin of victory in a major golf tournament since Tom Morris, Senior, won the 1862 (that's right, *1862!*) British Open by 13 shots.

14

1910 A baseball tradition began today. At the Washington Senators' game against Philadelphia, President William Howard Taft became the first U.S. President to throw out the ceremonial first pitch of a ball game.

1968 Roberto de Vicenzo learned never to sign a piece of paper without reading it first. The golfer shot a final-round 65 at the Masters, to force a playoff with Bob Goalby. But Roberto's scorecard had a math mistake in it: It said his score was 66. When Roberto signed the scorecard, 66 became his official score! They didn't have a playoff after all. Bob won.

1989 Riding his motorcycle, daredevil Robbie Knievel jumped the Caesars Palace fountain, in Las Vegas, Nevada. Robbie's dad, Evel Knievel, tried but failed to jump the fountain 22 years earlier.

1996 The Detroit Red Wings defeated the Dallas Stars, 5–1, in the last game of the NHL season. The victory was the team's 62nd of the season, an NHL record.

Birthdays

13•DANA BARROS, basketball (1967)

14•GREG MADDUX, baseball (1966)

15•ANTHONY MILLER, football (1965)

16•KAREEM ABDUL-JABBAR, basketball (1947)

15

1947 Jackie Robinson became the first black player in modern major league baseball. The Brooklyn Dodger was taunted by prejudiced fans and players all season long. It didn't keep Jackie from succeeding on the field — he batted .297 and was Rookie of the Year.

1965 The Philadelphia 76ers trailed the Boston Celtics, 110–109, in Game 7 of the Eastern Division final. The 76ers had the ball with five seconds to go. But Hal Greer's pass was deflected by Boston's John Havlicek. The Celtics went on to win their seventh-straight NBA title.

April 14, 1989: Robbie Knievel makes a daring jump on his motorcycle.

1991 In a game against Dallas, Magic Johnson recorded his 9,888th career assist. That put the Los Angeles Laker point guard ahead of Oscar Robertson as the NBA's all-time assist leader.

16

1912 A 28-year-old American named Harriet Quimby became the first woman to fly an airplane across the English Channel. The Channel is a famous 21-mile stretch of water between England and France. Harriet was also the first American woman to earn a pilot's license.

1988 Record times for men and women were set in a downhill ski competition at Les Arcs, France. Michael Pruffer of France zipped along at 139 miles per hour (m.p.h.). Tara Mulari of Finland was clocked at a speed of 133 m.p.h.

1994 Barry Bonds of the San Francisco Giants hit a two-run homer off Ryan Bowen at Florida's Joe Robbie Stadium today. With that shot, Barry had homered in every National League ballpark.

17

1953 New York Yankee Mickey Mantle hit the longest home run on record for a regular-season game. The record-setting homer was a 565-foot blast. The ball left Griffith Stadium, in Washington, D.C., and landed in somebody's back yard! (Seven years later, Mickey will shatter his own record with a towering 643-foot shot.)

1972 For the first time in its 76-year history, the Boston Marathon held a women's competition. Women raced beside the men, but their ranks and times were kept separate. The first winner in the women's division was Nina Kuscsik of Huntington, New York. She finished the 26-mile race in 3 hours, 8 minutes, 58 seconds.

1987 Julius Erving became the third player in basketball history to score 30,000 career points. Only Wilt Chamberlain and Kareem Abdul-Jabbar have scored more. Doctor J played for the New York Nets in the American Basketball Association before he joined the NBA's Philadelphia 76ers.

18

1945 Pete Gray, an outfielder for the St. Louis Browns, played in his first major league game today. The Browns beat Detroit, 7–1. Pete, who had just one arm, went one-for-four in his first game and batted .218 in his only big-league season.

1991 John Stockton of the Utah Jazz set a new NBA single-season assist record (1,164), breaking his own record of 1,134. John has the top three single-season assist totals in NBA history.

1994 Uta Pippig of Germany won the Boston Marathon in record time today. Uta crossed the finish line in 2 hours, 21 minutes, 45 seconds. She broke Joan Benoit's 11-year-old record.

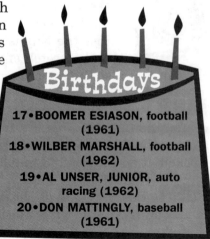

Birthdays

17•BOOMER ESIASON, football (1961)

18•WILBER MARSHALL, football (1962)

19•AL UNSER, JUNIOR, auto racing (1962)

20•DON MATTINGLY, baseball (1961)

APRIL

19

1897 The first Boston Marathon was held today. A New Yorker named John J. McDermott won with a time of 2 hours, 55 minutes, 10 seconds. The Boston Marathon was the first marathon ever held in the U.S. It was the only one of its kind until New York City held *its* first marathon in 1970.

1986 Dominique Wilkins of the Atlanta Hawks scored 50 points to tie a team playoff record. He led his team to a first-round win over the Detroit Pistons. Dominique had won the NBA regular-season-scoring title with an average of 30.3 points-per-game.

1991 Heavyweight champion Evander Holyfield kept his title by beating George Foreman. George, who was 42 years old and weighed more than 250 pounds, did not win the fight, but he did win the hearts of many Americans.

20

1985 Karyn Tarter Marshall lifted 303 pounds in a weightlifting move called a clean and jerk. It was the most weight ever lifted overhead by a woman. Karyn has won U.S. national championships five times.

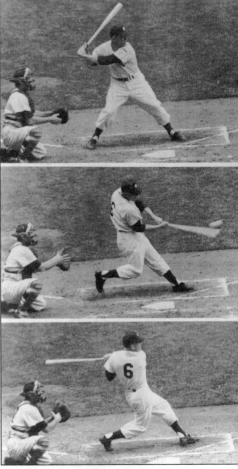

April 17, 1953: Mickey Mantle smacks a 565-foot homer!

1986 Michael Jordan scored 63 points against the Boston Celtics in Game 2 of the Eastern Conference playoffs. It was a playoff record. Despite Michael's scoring (he made 22 of 41 shots and 19 of 21 free throws), the Chicago Bulls lost in double-overtime, 135–131.

1993 The San Francisco 49ers traded quarterback Joe Montana to the Kansas City Chiefs. Joe had led the 49ers to four Super Bowl victories and was named MVP in three of them.

21

1980 Bill Rodgers won his third-straight Boston Marathon, but Rosie Ruiz stole the show. No one had ever heard of Rosie. Yet she was the first woman to cross the finish line. That made some people suspicious. It turned out, Rosie cheated. She had not run the whole race and was disqualified.

1991 John Harkes became the first American-born soccer player to play in an English League Cup championship. He helped his team, Sheffield Wednesday, win the English League Cup. The Kearny, New Jersey, native would not play pro soccer in the United States until 1996, when Major League Soccer started.

1996 The Chicago Bulls finished the NBA's 1995–96 regular season with a 103–93 win over the Washington Bullets (now called the Wizards). The victory gave the Bulls a record of 72 wins and only 10 losses for the 1995–96 season, the best single-season record in NBA history. The previous mark, 69–13, was set by the Los Angeles Lakers in 1971–72.

22

1954 The NBA adopted the 24-second clock, to make teams shoot more quickly. Danny Biasone, who owned the Syracuse Nationals, came up with the idea. Why 24 seconds? Because 2,880 seconds (the number of seconds in a game) divided by 120 (the number of shots two teams usually take in a game) equals 24.

1970 New York Met Tom Seaver struck out 19 batters in a 2–1 win over the San Diego Padres. It tied a record. Tom struck out the last 10 batters in a row, setting another record.

1994 Boxer Michael Moorer outpointed Evander Holyfield to win the heavyweight champion-ship by a decision today. Michael became the sixth heavyweight boxing champion since 1990.

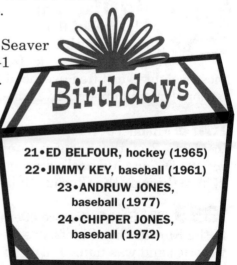

Birthdays

21•ED BELFOUR, hockey (1965)
22•JIMMY KEY, baseball (1961)
23•ANDRUW JONES, baseball (1977)
24•CHIPPER JONES, baseball (1972)

APRIL

 **1950** The NBA (National Basketball Association) held its first championship today. The Minneapolis Lakers beat the Syracuse Nationals, 110–95.

1989 Kareem Abdul-Jabbar scored more points than any player in NBA history. Today, he scored 10 points in his final regular-season game to help the Los Angeles Lakers beat the Seattle SuperSonics.

April 21, 1996: The Bulls win their 72nd game of the season to set an NBA record.

1991 Christophe Auguin of France won the BOC Challenge, a 27,000-mile sailing race around the world. Christophe was alone at sea for seven months.

 **1909** Harry L. Hillman and Lawson Robertson set a world record in the three-legged race. They ran 100 yards in 11 seconds — with one of each man's legs tied to one of the other man's legs!

1994 David Robinson of the San Antonio Spurs scored 71 points and won the NBA scoring title. Only Wilt Chamberlain, Elgin Baylor, and David Thompson have also scored 70 or more points in an NBA game.

1994 Mahmoud Abdul-Rauf of the Denver Nuggets had a chance to break Calvin Murphy's single-season free throw shooting record of 95.8 percent. Calvin was sitting courtside. Before Mahmoud's first attempt in the third quarter, Calvin rubbed the ball. Mahmoud made his first attempt but missed his second. Calvin's record stood.

1996 The Minnesota Twins clobbered the Detroit Tigers, 24–11. There were other football-style scores in the first month of the baseball season: The Texas Rangers crushed the Baltimore Orioles, 26–7, and the Montreal Expos mauled the Colorado Rockies, 21–9.

25 **1964** Today, the Toronto Maple Leafs won the Stanley Cup championship. They defeated the Detroit Red Wings to win their third straight Stanley Cup! (The Leafs would win the Cup again in 1967.)

1965 The Boston Celtics outscored the Los Angeles Lakers, 129–96, to win the NBA championship. L.A.'s Jerry West scored 33 points in today's game to set a new playoff record by scoring 447 points in 11 games. That's an average of 40.6 points per game.

1994 Florida State quarterback Charlie Ward couldn't decide whether he wanted to play pro football or basketball. So he became the first Heisman Trophy winner *not* to be selected in the NFL draft. When Charlie finally chose basketball, he was picked by the New York Knicks in the first round of the *NBA* draft.

1997 Seattle Mariner slugger Ken Griffey, Junior, smacked three home runs in a game against the Toronto Blue Jays. His first two homers were hit against Blue Jay ace Roger Clemens.

26 **1964** It was a good news/bad news game for Houston Astro pitcher Ken Johnson. The good news was that Ken threw a no-hitter against the Cincinnati Reds. The bad news was that he lost the game! Ken gave up the winning run in the ninth inning after he and his second baseman made errors.

1992 Golfer Davis Love III won the Greater Greensboro Open today. It was the third tournament title he had won in five weeks! But it was the *last* title Davis would win for the rest of the year.

1992 The Indianapolis Colts had the first two picks of the NFL draft today. The Colts selected defensive tackle Steve Emtman of Washington, as the number-one pick, and linebacker Quentin Coryatt of Texas A&M, as the number-two pick.

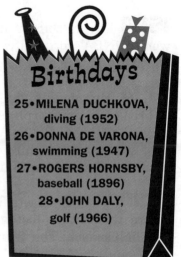

Birthdays

25•MILENA DUCHKOVA, diving (1952)

26•DONNA DE VARONA, swimming (1947)

27•ROGERS HORNSBY, baseball (1896)

28•JOHN DALY, golf (1966)

27

1956 Heavyweight boxing champion Rocky Marciano retired from the ring today. Rocky went out a winner. He is the only heavyweight champion in history to win every one of his professional fights. His 49 victories in 49 fights remains a record.

1983 Houston Astro fireballer Nolan Ryan struck out Montreal Expo Brad Mills to become baseball's all-time strikeout leader. Brad was Nolan's 3,508th strikeout victim. Nolan passed Walter Johnson, who had set the record in 1927.

April 27, 1983: Nolan Ryan is baseball's all-time strikeout leader.

1994 The sixth-longest game in NHL history was played today. It was Game 6 of the Eastern Conference quarterfinal series, between the Buffalo Sabres and New Jersey Devils. Buffalo's Dave Hannan scored at 5:43 of the fourth overtime period. The Sabres won, 1–0. The game, which began at 7:39 P.M., ended at 1:51 in the morning!

28

1966 The Boston Celtics beat out the Los Angeles Lakers for the NBA championship *again!* Boston took today's seventh and deciding game, 95–93. The victory gave the Celtics a record eight-straight championships.

1988 The Baltimore Orioles got off to the worst start in baseball history. When the Minnesota Twins beat them today, the Orioles' record dropped to 0–21 — an American League record for consecutive losses. The Orioles will finish the season in last place.

1995 The Boston Celtics suffered the worst playoff loss in franchise history. The 124–77 defeat came in Game 1 of their series against the Orlando Magic. But the Celtics rebounded in Game 2 with a 99–92 victory. They became the first Eastern Conference team to beat the Magic at Orlando Arena this season.

29

1961 ABC-TV's *Wide World of Sports* hit the airwaves for the first time. It began as a 20-week series. The show is now one of the longest-running sports programs in the history of television.

1981 Philadelphia Phillie pitcher Steve Carlton became the first left-hander in major league history to strike out 3,000 batters. He fanned Tim Wallach of the Montreal Expos in the first inning for number 3,000. In all, "Lefty" Carlton struck out nine Expos on his way to a 6–2 victory.

1986 Roger Clemens of the Boston Red Sox struck out 20 batters today — a major league record for a nine-inning game.

30

1969 Jim Maloney of the Cincinnati Reds struck out 13 Houston Astros in today's game. He didn't allow one Astro to get a hit, either! It was Jim's third career no-hitter.

1971 The Milwaukee Bucks won the NBA title in their third year of existence. Before the season, the Bucks had traded for Oscar Robertson. He teamed with Lew Alcindor (who will change his name to Kareem Abdul-Jabbar). Together, they led Milwaukee to a 12–2 record in the playoffs.

1986 One if by land, two if by *somersault?* Ashrita Furman set a somersaulting record today. Ashrita tumbled along the route of Paul Revere's historic ride. It took more than 10 hours, and Ashrita did 8,341 somersaults.

1994 The San Jose Sharks took a bite out of the Detroit Red Wings. The Sharks knocked the Central Division champs out of the playoffs by winning Game 7 of their first-round series. The Sharks had never been in the playoffs before.

Birthdays

29•ANDRE AGASSI, tennis (1970)

29•DALE EARNHARDT, auto racer (1952)

30•ISIAH THOMAS, basketball (1961)

30•DAVE MEGGETT, football (1966)

MAY

May 30, 1982: Cal Ripken, Junior, begins his "Iron Man" streak.

1

1884 Who was the first black player in major league baseball? Jackie Robinson? Nope. On this day, 63 years before Jackie made baseball history, an African-American catcher named Moses Fleetwood Walker played his first game for the Toledo (Ohio) club in a major league called the American Association. Since blacks will be banned from the majors for many years, Jackie gets credit for breaking the color barrier.

1991 Nolan Ryan of the Texas Rangers pitched a no-hitter against the Toronto Blue Jays. It was the seventh no-hitter of his 26-year career — a major league record. Nolan struck out Roberto Alomar for the final out. Roberto's father, Sandy, was Nolan's teammate when he pitched his first no-hitter, back in 1973.

1991 Oakland A's speedster Rickey Henderson stole his 939th base today, in a game against the New York Yankees. With that stolen base, Rickey became baseball's leading base thief.

2

1917 Fred Toney of the Cincinnati Reds and Hippo Vaughn of the Chicago Cubs both pitched nine no-hit innings — in the same game! It was the first double no-hitter in history. Hippo's arm gave out first. He gave up two hits in the 10th inning and lost the game.

1939 New York Yankee great Lou Gehrig did not play today. It was the first game the "Iron Man" missed since June 6, 1925. The streak of 2,130 games was a major league record that stood for 56 years. (Baltimore's Cal Ripken, Junior, will break Lou's record on September 6, 1995.)

1992 Lil E. Tee was born so sickly that he almost died. The colt grew up healthy, but was still a long shot to win the Kentucky Derby. His jockey, Pat Day, had never won the race before. Pat's luck changed today and Lil E. Tee ran to victory.

Birthdays

1•GARY CLARK, baseball (1962)

2•RUSS GRIMM, golf (1928)

3•SUGAR RAY ROBINSON, boxing (1921)

4•DAWN STALEY, basketball (1970)

3

1986 Bill Shoemaker became the oldest jockey ever to win the Kentucky Derby. The 54-year-old rode Ferdinand to victory. It was Bill's fourth Derby win.

1994 Charles Barkley scored 56 points in today's first-round playoff game between the Phoenix Suns and the Golden State Warriors. The scoring explosion was a career high for Charles and the third-highest total in NBA playoff history! (Michael Jordan holds the record with 63, and Elgin Baylor is second with 61.)

May 4, 1929: Yankee slugger Lou Gehrig hits three home runs in three at-bats.

1994 Chris Webber of the Golden State Warriors won the NBA Rookie of the Year award. Chris was the first rookie ever to total more than 1,000 points, 500 rebounds, 250 assists, 150 blocks, and 75 steals in a season.

4

1929 New York Yankee slugger Lou Gehrig had a sizzling game against the Detroit Tigers today. In three straight at-bats, Lou pounded out three straight home runs. Lou's slugging helped New York edge Detroit, 11–9.

1968 The first American Basketball Association (ABA) championship was held. The Pittsburgh Pipers nipped the New Orleans Buccaneers, four games to three. The league will fold in 1977, but four of its teams will join the NBA: the New Jersey Nets, Denver Nuggets, Indiana Pacers, and San Antonio Spurs.

1975 Bob Watson of the Houston Astros scored the one-millionth run in major league baseball history. Bob was on base when teammate Milt May cracked a home run.

5

1904 Cy Young of the Boston Red Sox pitched a perfect game today. He didn't allow any hits or walks in Boston's 3–0 defeat of the Philadelphia Phillies. It was the first perfect game since the pitcher's mound had been moved to it's current distance from the plate — 60 feet, 6 inches.

1969 *Not again!* For the seventh time in 11 years, the Los Angeles Lakers lost the NBA championship to the Boston Celtics. They lost the seventh game of the finals to Boston, 108–106. (It was Boston's 10th championship in 11 years!)

1978 Pete Rose of the Cincinnati Reds got the 3,000th base hit of his career. Not only was Pete the 13th player to reach that mark, but at age 37, he was also the youngest. By the time he retired, Pete will have an incredible 4,256 hits — more than any other baseball player in major league history.

6

1953 It's not how you start, it's how you finish. Making his first major league start for the St. Louis Browns, Bobo Holloman pitched a no-hitter against the Philadelphia A's. But Bobo ended the year with a disappointing 3–7 record and never pitched in the big leagues again.

1954 Running a mile in less than four minutes seemed impossible to most people, but not to Roger Bannister. On a cold, windy day in England, Roger crossed the finish line in 3 minutes, 59.4 seconds — a world record.

1982 Gaylord Perry helped the Seattle Mariners beat the New York Yankees, for the 300th victory of his career. Gaylord is the only pitcher to win the Cy Young Award in both leagues. He won a lot of games by throwing spitballs, which are illegal in the major leagues. (After he retires, Gaylord will admit to having thrown a few spitballs.)

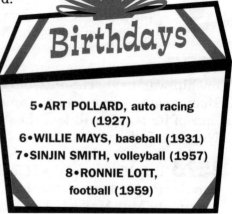

Birthdays

5•ART POLLARD, auto racing (1927)
6•WILLIE MAYS, baseball (1931)
7•SINJIN SMITH, volleyball (1957)
8•RONNIE LOTT, football (1959)

MAY

7 **1972** Some things are worth the wait. After losing eight NBA Finals, the Los Angeles Lakers won the championship! They rolled over the New York Knicks in five games.

1994 Until today, every NCAA men's volleyball champion had come from California. Penn State University ended that tradition. The Nittany Lions spiked the defending UCLA champions, 3–2.

May 6, 1954: Roger Bannister runs a mile in less than four minutes!

1995 It was one of the most stunning comebacks in NBA playoff history. Reggie Miller of the Indiana Pacers scored the game's final 8 points in the last 16.4 seconds! His effort helped the Pacers edge the New York Knicks, 107–105, in Game 1 of the Eastern Conference semi-finals. The Pacers won the series in seven games.

8 **1963** The worst batting slump in baseball history came to an end today. After 88 at-bats without a hit, pitcher Bob Buhl of the Chicago Cubs connected for a single.

1970 After 24 years in the league, the New York Knicks won their first NBA championship. They earned the title by defeating the Los Angeles Lakers in seven games. The Knicks won the championship again three years later. They haven't done it since.

1994 Scoring sensation Pavel Bure of the Vancouver Canucks netted an overtime goal to power the Canucks to a 2–1 victory over the Dallas Stars and a 3–1 series lead in the NHL playoffs. The win stretched the Canucks' playoff record in overtime to 4–0. They had beaten the Calgary Flames in three-straight overtime games to win their first-round series.

9

1961 Jim Gentile of the Baltimore Orioles used his bat to make baseball history. Playing against the Minnesota Twins, the first baseman pounded a home run with the bases loaded in the first inning. Then he did it again in the second inning. Jim set a major league record by knocking in eight runs in two at-bats!

1992 Terry Norris, the WBC super welterweight champion, defended his title against Meldrick Taylor, the WBA welterweight champion. Terry entered the ring with the word KNOCKOUT shaved on the back of his head. He used his hands as well as his head and knocked out Meldrick in the fourth round!

1993 The Phoenix Suns made one of the best comebacks in NBA history. After losing two playoff games at home, the Suns stormed back to defeat the Los Angeles Lakers for the third straight time and win their first-round playoff series!

10

1970 Hockey great Bobby Orr scored an overtime goal in Game 4 of the Stanley Cup finals. The goal won the game and clinched the Cup for the Boston Bruins. It was their first championship in 29 years.

1992 Race-car driver A.J. Foyt qualified for the Indianapolis 500 for the 35th year in a row — a record. A.J., who had won the Indy 500 four times, is the all-time leader in Indy Car victories, with 67.

1994 Carol Blazejowski made it into the Naismith Memorial Basketball Hall of Fame today. When women's college basketball began to take off in the 1970's, Carol was one of its brightest stars. "The Blaze" was an outstanding scorer for Montclair State College, in New Jersey. In three seasons, Carol scored 3,199 points. That's an average of 31.7 points per game!

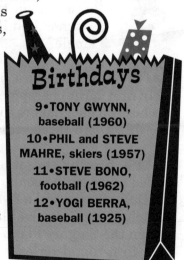

Birthdays

9•TONY GWYNN, baseball (1960)

10•PHIL and STEVE MAHRE, skiers (1957)

11•STEVE BONO, football (1962)

12•YOGI BERRA, baseball (1925)

11

1955 Ernie Banks helped to end the Brooklyn Dodgers' 11-game winning streak today. He smacked a grand slam to help the Chicago Cubs clip the Brooklyn Dodgers, 10–8. It was Ernie's first grand slam of the season. He will finish the year with five!

1977 After his team lost 16 straight games, Atlanta Braves owner Ted Turner took over as manager today. But the Braves still lost! The National League then ruled that owners may not manage their teams.

May 12, 1979: Chris Evert's amazing 125-match winning streak comes to an end.

1994 Isiah Thomas of the Detroit Pistons announced his retirement from basketball today. Though he is only only 6' 1" and 185 pounds (small for an NBA player), Isiah proved that he could succeed in a big man's game. The point guard captained the Pistons to two NBA championships in 1989 and 1990.

12

1979 "The Streak" came to an end today. Chris Evert had won 125 matches in a row on clay courts. Today, she took her first loss since August 12, 1973: Tracy Austin beat Chris in three sets at the Italian Open.

1982 The United States Football League was founded today. The league plays its games in the spring. It will last four years.

1985 Kathy Whitworth won the United Virginia Bank Classic for her 88th and final victory on the Ladies Professional Golf Association tour. Kathy won more titles than any other golfer. She also won the Vare Trophy for best scoring average seven times.

MAY

13

1983 Baseball slugger Reggie Jackson became the first player to strike out 2,000 times. The free-swinging outfielder will whiff a total of 2,597 times in his 21-year career. If the strikeouts had come one right after the other, Reggie could have gone about four seasons without a hit!

1994 California Angel rightfielder Tim Salmon hit two home runs, two singles, and a double. That gave him 13 hits in his last three games, tying an American League record. During the streak, Tim upped his average from .272 to .336!

1994 With 1.8 seconds remaining in an NBA playoff game, the Chicago Bulls and New York Knicks were tied, 102–102. The Bulls called a time out and planned a play for Toni Kukoc to take the last shot. He did . . . and scored! The Bulls won the game, 104–102.

14

1972 Willie Mays played his first game as a New York Met — and cracked the game-winning home run! The Mets defeated Willie's old team, the San Francisco Giants, 5–4. Willie is near the end of a great career, in which he hit 660 home runs. He will help lead the Mets to the World Series the following year, and then retire.

1993 The New York Islanders became Patrick Division champions today. The Isles scored an overtime goal in the seventh game of the division final, upsetting the Stanley Cup champion Pittsburgh Penguins. David Volek scored the game-winning goal.

1995 The Phoenix Suns beat the Houston Rockets in Game 4 of the Western Conference Finals. The win gave the Suns a 3–1 series lead. But Houston will bounce back, burning the Suns in three straight to clinch the series. (The Rockets will go on to win their second-straight championship.)

Birthdays

13•DENNIS RODMAN, basketball (1961)
14•DENNIS MARTINEZ, baseball (1955)
15•EMMITT SMITH, football (1969)
16•GABRIEL SABATINI, tennis (1970)

82

15

1941 Joe DiMaggio, of the New York Yankees, hit a single off Chicago White Sox pitcher Edgar Smith. With that base hit, "The Yankee Clipper" started what will become a major league record 56-game hitting streak.

1984 The Los Angeles Lakers defeated the Phoenix Suns, 118–102, in the NBA playoffs. Laker point guard Magic Johnson recorded 24 assists, an NBA playoff record. (On May 17, 1988, Utah's John Stockton will tie the record in a playoff game against Magic and the Lakers.)

May 15, 1941: New York Yankee Joe DiMaggio kicks off his 56-game hitting streak.

1990 The Edmonton Oilers beat the Boston Bruins, 3–2, in the longest game in Stanley Cup history. Peter Klima hit the winning goal in triple overtime in Game 1 of the Stanley Cup finals.

16

1903 George A. Wyman revved up his motorcycle in San Francisco, California, and started a road trip. He wanted to become the first man to cross the U.S. on a motorbike. On July 6, he will arrive in New York City.

1980 The Los Angeles Lakers led the Philadelphia 76ers three games to two in the NBA Finals, but they had a problem: Laker center Kareem Abdul-Jabbar was hurt. So rookie Magic Johnson stepped in to play center. Magic, who is 6' 9" tall, made 42 points, 15 rebounds, and 7 assists to lead the Lakers to the NBA title.

1993 Raul Alcala of Mexico clinched the Tour du Pont bicycle race. He won the 36.5-mile time trial, beating Lance Armstrong of the U.S. in the overall standings by 2 minutes, 26 seconds.

MAY

 **1970** Hank Aaron stroked his 3,000th career hit in a game against the San Francisco Giants. But he was just getting started! In his next at-bat, the rightfielder slammed career home run number 500! Hank, Willie Mays, and Eddie Murray are the only players to collect more than 3,000 hits and 500 career homers.

1979 The Philadelphia Phillies outlasted the Chicago White Sox, 23–22, in a crazy baseball game in Chicago. The teams combined for 50 hits, including 11 home runs. Future Hall of Famer Mike Schmidt hit a game-winning homer in the 10th inning.

1983 The New York Islanders beat the Edmonton Oilers, 4–2, to complete a four-game sweep in the Stanley Cup final. It has been a good decade for the Islanders so far. They have won the Stanley Cup four times in four seasons.

1929 Johnny Frederick of the Brooklyn Dodgers set a National League record for most runs scored in a double-header. He scored five times in the first game and three times in the second against the Philadelphia Phillies.

1986 Pat Bradley became the first woman golfer to top $2 million in career earnings. Pat will win five LPGA titles, including three major championships, in 1986. She will also take Player of the Year honors and the Vare Trophy for low scoring average.

1992 For the second straight year and third time in his career, Michael Jordan was named the NBA's Most Valuable Player. The Chicago Bull guard joined Magic Johnson, Larry Bird, and Moses Malone as three-time MVP winners.

1996 Soccer forward Michelle Akers scored to lift the U.S. to a 1–0 win over China and the U.S. Women's World Cup title. She is named tournament MVP.

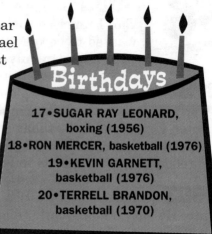

Birthdays

17•SUGAR RAY LEONARD, boxing (1956)

18•RON MERCER, basketball (1976)

19•KEVIN GARNETT, basketball (1976)

20•TERRELL BRANDON, basketball (1970)

19

1974 Singer Kate Smith was the Philadelphia Flyers' good-luck charm. Whenever the Flyers needed a big win, she would sing "God Bless America" before the game. With Kate at the microphone, the Flyers had a record of 36–3–1! So in the seventh game of the Stanley Cup final, Kate sang again. The Flyers won the game and the championship.

1984 One dynasty ended, but another one started. The Edmonton Oilers won the Stanley Cup over the New York Islanders, ending New

May 20, 1989: Sunday Silence *(left)* **noses out Easy Goer in the Preakness Stakes.**

York's streak at four titles in a row. The Oilers will skate off with five championships in seven seasons.

1991 Willy T. Ribbs became the first African-American auto racer to qualify for the Indianapolis 500. He was sponsored by comedian Bill Cosby. Willy finished the race in 32nd place.

20

1988 Rodeo rider Lane Frost did what no other man could do. He stayed on a bucking bull named Red Rock for a full eight seconds! Since 1980, that bull had thrown 312 riders in a row.

1989 It was the closest Preakness Stakes race ever. Sunday Silence and Easy Goer ran side by side, neck and neck. At the finish line, it was Sunday Silence — the winner by a nose. For the first time since 1978, the Preakness ended in a photo finish.

1993 Lisa Raymond of the University of Florida beat North Carolina's Cinda Gurney to win her second-straight NCAA women's tennis title. Lisa now competes on the pro tour.

21

1819 One of the first bicycles in the U.S. was seen in New York. Early bikes were called velocipedes (from the word *velocity*, meaning "speed"). They were not speedy, though. They had huge wheels and were hard to control.

1979 With future Hall of Famers Ken Dryden in goal and Guy Lafleur cruising on right wing, the Montreal Canadiens won their fourth straight Stanley Cup. They beat the New York Rangers in five games. (Montreal has won the most Stanley Cups ever: 24.)

1994 After losing the first two playoff games of their series with the Phoenix Suns at home, the Houston Rockets fired back. They won the series in seven games. Rookie guard Sam Cassell scored 22 points and added seven assists to lead the Rockets to victory in Game 7. Houston won, 104–94.

22

1988 NBA superstars Larry Bird and Dominique Wilkins battled it out in Game 7 of the playoff series between the Boston Celtics and Atlanta Hawks. Dominique scored a game-high 47 points for Atlanta, and Larry scored 34 points for Boston, including 20 in the fourth quarter. The Celtics won, 118–116, to advance to the next round.

1992 The Chicago Blackhawks made it to the Stanley Cup finals for the first time since 1973. They beat Edmonton, 5–1, completing a sweep of the Oilers. The win gave Chicago its 11th straight playoff win, an NHL single-season record.

1994 The Chicago Bulls had eliminated the Knicks from the playoffs two years in a row. Today, the Knicks turned things around. They knocked off the three-time defending champion Bulls in Game 7 of the Eastern Conference semi-finals, 87–77.

Birthdays

21•KENT HRBEK, baseball (1960)
22•HORTON SMITH, golf (1908)
23•MARVIN HAGLER, boxing (1954)
24•JOE DUMARS, basketball (1963)
24•LIZ McCOLGAN, track and field (1964)

23 **1977** Jockey Steve Cauthen was hurt in a three-horse accident at Belmont Park, in New York City. The 17-year-old jockey suffered a broken wrist and cracked ribs in the spill. Even though he missed a month of racing, "The Kid" will win 487 races during the year.

1982 The Philadelphia 76ers became the NBA's Eastern Conference champions by crushing their rivals, the Boston Celtics. Philly's top player, Julius Erving, averaged 19 points, seven rebounds, and four assists per game in the series.

1993 For the second-straight year, the Orlando Magic won the top pick in the NBA draft lottery. At the NBA draft, on June 30, Orlando will draft Chris Webber, then trade him to the Golden State Warriors for Anfernee "Penny" Hardaway and first-round picks in 1996, 1998, and 2000.

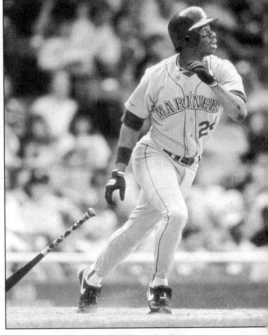

May 24, 1994: Ken Griffey, Junior, sets a record with his 21st homer.

24 **1990** The Edmonton Oilers won their fifth Stanley Cup in seven years. Goaltender Bill Ranford allowed the Boston Bruins just eight goals in the five-game Stanley Cup final series to earn MVP honors.

1992 Auto racing runs in the family of Al Unser, Junior. His father, Al Senior, has won the Indy 500 four times and his uncle Bobby has won three times. Today Al junior added an Indy win of his own. He nosed out Scott Goodyear to win the big race by less than one second! It was the closest finish ever at the Indy 500.

1994 Seattle Mariner superstar Ken Griffey, Junior, hit his 21st home run of the season. With that blast, Ken broke Mickey Mantle's record for most homers in the first two months of a season.

25

1965 Muhammad Ali flattened Sonny Liston in the first round to retain his heavyweight title and prove that his fists move as fast as his mouth. Muhammad challenged Sonny to get up and fight. He didn't.

1975 The Golden State Warriors dodged the Washington Bullets, 96–95, to sweep the NBA championship in four games. It was only the third sweep in NBA Finals history.

1991 Pittsburgh Penguin center Mario Lemieux led the Penguins to their first Stanley Cup title in their history. "Super Mario" was awarded the Conn Smythe Trophy as the MVP of the playoffs. He played in five of the six games of the finals, scoring five goals and seven assists.

1994 With his team trailing three games to two in a playoff series, New York Ranger captain Mark Messier promised that his team would beat the New Jersey Devils in Game 6. Mark scored three third-period goals to gain a 4–2 victory and force a seventh game.

26

1976 It was a baseball pitching matchup that pitted brother against brother. Joe Niekro was on the mound for the Houston Astros and his older brother Phil was on the mound for the Atlanta Braves. The Astros beat the Braves, 4–1, and Joe smacked a home run off his brother.

1991 Rick Mears won the Indianapolis 500 today. He drove at an average speed of 176 miles per hour for 200 laps! Rick, who also won in 1979, 1984, and 1988, joined A.J. Foyt and Al Unser, Senior, as the only four-time winners of Indy racing's biggest event.

1994 Lenny Wilkens of the Atlanta Hawks was named NBA Coach of the Year. Lenny had become the NBA's all-time winningest coach, breaking Red Auerbach's record of 938 victories.

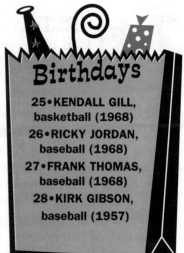

Birthdays

25•KENDALL GILL, basketball (1968)

26•RICKY JORDAN, baseball (1968)

27•FRANK THOMAS, baseball (1968)

28•KIRK GIBSON, baseball (1957)

27

1896 Columbia University was the easy winner of the first inter-collegiate bicycle meet. Five races were held in Brooklyn, New York.

1937 Pitcher Carl Hubbell of the New York Giants extended his major league-record winning streak to 24 games. Carl, who played for the Giants from 1928 to 1943, won 253 games during his career.

May. 26. 1991: Rick Mears powers into first place at the Indianapolis 500.

1975 The Philadelphia Flyers defeated the Buffalo Sabres in six games to win their second straight Stanley Cup title. Flyer captain Bobby Clarke was named the regular-season Most Valuable Player. But it was goaltender Bernie Parent who sparkled during the playoffs, becoming the first player ever to be named playoff MVP two straight years.

28

1951 Willie Mays, the rookie centerfielder of the New York Giants, was in a terrible slump. He was hitless in his first 26 at-bats in the major leagues. He even asked his manager, Leo Durocher, to send him down to the minors. Leo refused, and Willie got his confidence back. He went out and got his first hit today. It was a home run!

1976 Ron LeFlore's 30-game hitting streak came to an end today. During a game against the New York Yankees, the Detroit Tiger failed to get a hit. It was the first time since April 17 he had gone hitless. During that stretch of time, Ron had batted .392 with 51 hits in 130 at bats.

1994 Princeton University won the men's NCAA Division I lacrosse title for the second time in three years. The Tigers beat Virginia, 9–8, in overtime. The win completed a sweep for the school. The women's team had won the NCAA title the week before!

29

1977 Janet Guthrie became the first woman to race in the Indianapolis 500. She had qualified with an average speed of 188 miles per hour! Unfortunately, Janet's car broke down during the race.

1992 The Minnesota Vikings released running back Herschel Walker. Minnesota had picked him up three years ago in one of the worst trades in NFL history. In exchange for Herschel, the Vikings had sent the Dallas Cowboys five players and eight draft choices. Based on the trade, Dallas built two Super Bowl champions.

1994 The Atlanta Braves traded two-sport star Deion Sanders to the Cincinnati Reds for Roberto Kelly.

1994 Al Unser, Junior, won the Indianapolis 500 for the second time in three years. By year's end, "Little Al" will win seven more Indy-car races and the driving title.

30

1982 Today, Cal Ripken, Junior, of the Baltimore Orioles began his consecutive-games-played streak. Cal, who started at third base in a game against Toronto, has not missed a game since. He will break Lou Gehrig's record of 2,130 straight games on September 6, 1995.

1992 Georgia's Vicki Goetz won the NCAA women's golf championship, shooting the best 18 holes in the event's history. She made seven birdies en route to a final-round 65 at Arizona State University's Karsten Golf Course.

1994 The University of Arizona shut out Cal State-Northridge, 4–0, to win the NCAA Division I softball title for the second straight year. Wildcat pitcher Susie Parra allowed one hit and struck out 13.

Birthdays

29 • ERIC DAVIS, baseball (1962)

30 • GALE SAYERS, football (1943)

31 • JOE NAMATH, football (1943)

31 • KENNY LOFTON, baseball (1967)

31

1986 Auto racer Bobby Rahal set a record for the fastest Indianapolis 500. Bobby averaged almost 171 miles per hour and finished the race in 2 hours, 55 minutes, and 42 seconds. It was the first time in the 75-year history of the Indy 500 that anyone finished in less than 3 hours.

1991 The New York Knicks hired a familiar face to be the team's new coach. Pat Riley, who had won four NBA titles with the Los Angeles Lakers, came East with a mission — to win another NBA title for New York. Although Pat will come up one game short in the 1994 finals, his four-year stay with the Knicks will be successful. When he resigns after the 1994–95 season, Pat will have more playoff wins than any other coach in NBA history.

May 29, 1992: Minnesota releases former Heisman Trophy winner Herschel Walker.

1993 Arizona took advantage of an error by UCLA shortstop Kristy Howard to score the game's only run and win the College Softball World Series. Even though she lost the title game, UCLA's ace pitcher, Lisa Fernandez, finished her career with a record of 93–7.

1993 Syracuse won its fourth NCAA men's lacrosse title in six years, edging out North Carolina, 13–12, on Matt Riter's goal with eight seconds left to play. Syracuse goalie Chris Surran made 20 saves in the title game and was named MVP.

JUNE

June 7, 1997: Steve Yzerman and the Detroit Red Wings win the Stanley Cup!

1 **1986** Pat Bradley won the Ladies Professional Golf Association (LPGA) championship today. The victory made Pat the first to win all four of the top women's tournaments: the du Maurier Classic, the U.S. Open, the Dinah Shore, and the LPGA. On May 18, she had also become the first woman to earn more than $2 million in her golf career!

1992 The Pittsburgh Penguins downed the Chicago Blackhawks, 6–5, to sweep the series and win their second straight Stanley Cup title. The players dedicated their triumph to coach Bob Johnson. Bob had coached the Penguins to the 1990–91 title. He died in November 1991.

1993 Jim Pierce, father of tennis player Mary Pierce, was known for shouting at her opponents during matches. Today, he was ejected from the stands at the French Open. He was also banned from attending all future tennis tournaments.

1994 Reggie Miller caught fire in Game 5 of the Indiana Pacer's playoff series against the New York Knicks. Red-hot Reggie scored 25 of his game-high 39 points in the fourth quarter. Indiana won the game, 93–86, but the Knicks rebounded to win the series.

2 **1984** Patty Sheehan enjoyed one of the greatest rounds in women's golf today. She birdied eight of the first 13 holes and scored an eagle on 18. The next day she won her second straight LPGA title.

1990 Randy Johnson is 6' 10" tall. But today, Randy probably felt *ten* feet tall. He pitched the first no-hitter in Seattle Mariner history.

1991 Today's Milwaukee 200 Indy Car race was full of Andrettis. Michael, John, and Mario Andretti finished 1–2–3 in the race. (Michael and John are brothers. Mario is their father.)

Birthdays

1•PAUL COFFEY, hockey (1961)
1•ALAN AMECHE, football (1933)
2•PAULA NEWBY-FRASER, triathlon (1962)
2•SAM MILLS, football (1959)

3

1851 The New York Knickerbockers became the first baseball team to wear uniforms. Their outfits might seem a little strange if players wore them today. The Knickerbockers wore straw hats, white button-down shirts, and baggy blue pants!

1975 Pelé signed with the New York Cosmos of the North American Soccer League today. New York gave the soccer great a three-year, $7 million contract. The deal made Pelé the world's richest team athlete. Before he joined the Cosmos, the team averaged about 10,000 fans per game. By 1977, Pelé's last year with the team, attendance had soared to almost 35,000 per game.

1991 At age 32, Thomas Hearns was considered old for a boxer. "The Hit Man" hadn't knocked out an opponent in four years. Today, Thomas faced WBA light heavyweight champion Virgil Hill. He used his quick jab to defeat Virgil by a decision. For Thomas, it was his sixth title in 14 years.

4

1980 Gordie Howe retired after 32 years of playing pro hockey. He was 52 years old! "Mr. Hockey" played in the NHL and the World Hockey Association and set pro records by scoring 975 goals and 2,358 points.

1987 The longest winning streak in track and field history came to an end on this day. Edwin Moses had won the 400-meter hurdles race 122 times in a row. Today, Edwin lost to Danny Harris.

1989 In one of the greatest comebacks in tennis history, Michael Chang outlasted Ivan Lendl in the 16th round of the French Open. Michael's muscles were so sore that he was forced to serve underhand. At one point, he was two sets behind Ivan. But Michael stormed back to win the five-set struggle.

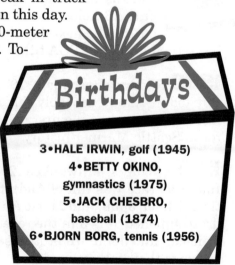

Birthdays

3 • HALE IRWIN, golf (1945)
4 • BETTY OKINO, gymnastics (1975)
5 • JACK CHESBRO, baseball (1874)
6 • BJORN BORG, tennis (1956)

5

1935 Strike three and the umpire's out! When the umpire in a Pacific Coast League game got sick, Oakland Oaks player Wee Willie Ludolph stepped in. And when the Oaks needed a pinch hitter, Willie stepped up to the plate. He struck out!

1993 Julie Krone became the first woman jockey to ride a winner in a Triple Crown race. She guided Colonial Affair to a win in the 125th Belmont Stakes.

June 3, 1975: Brazilian soccer great Pelé joins the New York Cosmos.

1994 Patrick Ewing of the New York Knicks slam-dunked a rebound with 27 seconds left in Game 7 of the NBA semi-finals against the Indiana Pacers. The Knicks defeated Indiana, 94–90, and reached the NBA Finals for the first time in 21 years.

6

1896 George Harbo and Frank Samuelson jumped into a boat and started to row across the Atlantic Ocean today. They made the trip from New York City to Le Havre, France, in 61 days!

1992 Arizona State University's Phil Mickelson won the NCAA men's golf championship for the third time. He crushed the runner-up, Harry Rudolph, by seven strokes. Phil is now on the PGA tour.

1992 Eddie Murray, the New York Mets' switch-hitting first baseman, knocked in the 1,510th run of his career today. With that crack of the bat, he passed Mickey Mantle to become major league baseball's career RBI leader among switch-hitters.

1992 Tennis star Monica Seles outplayed Steffi Graf to win the French Open. Monica became the first woman in 55 years to win three straight French Open titles.

1913 Hudson Stuck became the first man to climb Mount McKinley, in Alaska. Mount McKinley is the highest mountain in North America (20,320 feet). Hudson led a party of four men to the top of the mountain.

1992 American tennis ace Jim Courier beat Czechoslovakia's Petr Korda to win the French Open. After the final match, Jim charmed the crowd with his victory speech. He gave it in French!

1997 The Detroit Red Wings completed a four-game sweep of the Philadelphia Flyers to win their first Stanley Cup in 42 seasons! Goaltender Mike Vernon won the Conn Smythe Trophy as playoff MVP.

1961 The Milwaukee Braves hit four home runs in a row in the seventh inning in today's game. They still *lost* to the Cincinnati Reds, 10–8. Eddie Mathews, Hank Aaron, Joe Adcock, and Frank Thomas (not the White Sox first baseman) hit the Milwaukee home runs.

1966 The NFL announced that it would merge with its rival, the American Football League (AFL). Four years later, the NFL and AFL would become one league of two conferences: the National Football Conference (NFC) and the American Football Conference (AFC). Pete Rozelle would be chosen as the commissioner of the new league.

1968 Don Drysdale of the Los Angeles Dodgers pitched his way into the record books today. He extended his streak to 58⅔ innings in a row without giving up a single run!

1996 Louisiana State University (LSU) won the College World Series on a two-run homer by Warren Morris. The blast came on the game's final pitch and gave the Tigers a 9–8 victory over the University of Miami. It was the first time in the 50-year history of the College World Series that the championship has been decided by a home run!

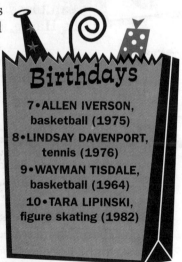

Birthdays

7 • ALLEN IVERSON, basketball (1975)

8 • LINDSAY DAVENPORT, tennis (1976)

9 • WAYMAN TISDALE, basketball (1964)

10 • TARA LIPINSKI, figure skating (1982)

9

1946 New York Giant manager Mel Ott was tossed out of the first game of a doubleheader today. (He was arguing with the umpire.) The Giants' skipper was ejected from the second game, too! Mel became the first major league manager to be thrown out of both ends of a doubleheader.

1973 Secretariat won the Belmont Stakes by an amazing 31 lengths! He became the first horse in 25 years to win racing's Triple Crown.

June 10, 1978: Affirmed nips Alydar in the Belmont Stakes and wins the Triple Crown!

1993 The U.S. men's soccer team pulled off an international shocker today. The team defeated England, 2–0, in a U.S. Cup match. Thomas Dooley scored the first goal on a header, and Alexi Lalas added the second goal. U.S. goalkeeper Tony Meola made 15 saves and was named the game's MVP.

10

1944 Joe Nuxhall of the Cincinnati Reds became the youngest pitcher ever to play in the majors. Joe was 15 when he pitched two thirds of an inning against the St. Louis Cardinals. He gave up five runs, five walks, and threw a wild pitch. Cincinnati lost, 18–0.

1978 At times during today's Belmont Stakes, Affirmed and Alydar looked like one horse. They galloped side by side, stride for stride. But in the end, Affirmed edged Alydar, winning the race — and the Triple Crown — by a nose.

1992 Mark McGwire of the Oakland A's hit his 200th career home run in his 2,852nd big-league at-bat. Mark became the fifth-fastest slugger to reach the 200-homer milestone. Only Ralph Kiner, Babe Ruth, Harmon Killebrew, and Eddie Mathews did it faster.

11

1977 Jockey Jean Cruguet rode Seattle Slew across the finish line to win the Belmont Stakes. With victories at the Kentucky Derby, the Preakness Stakes, and the Belmont, Seattle Slew became just the 10th thoroughbred in history to win the Triple Crown.

1978 Golfer Nancy Lopez won the LPGA Championship with a 13-under-par 275, six shots better than her closest competitor. She burst onto the golf scene this year to win nine tournaments, including a record five in a row. Nancy will win Player of the Year honors as a rookie.

1988 The Yankees had a strange starting lineup in a game against the Baltimore Orioles — the designated hitter was a pitcher! Rick Rhoden, who was a good-hitting pitcher, grounded out and drove in a run with a sacrifice fly in two at-bats.

12

1974 Little League baseball announced that girls would be allowed to play, too. On August 23, 1989, a girl will play in the Little League World Series for the first time. Victoria Bruckner scored three runs to help her team from San Pedro, California, win the championship.

1987 A team from the United States won the women's World Bowling Championships for the third year in a row. The American women set a record for most points scored in a game — 1,063.

1990 Oakland A's reliever Dennis Eckersley pitched his 52nd straight inning without allowing a walk. He faced 185 batters over that time!

1991 The Chicago Bulls became NBA champs for the first time. The Bulls knocked off the Los Angeles Lakers in five games.

Birthdays

11•JOE MONTANA, football (1956)

12•GWEN TORRENCE, track and field (1965)

13•RED GRANGE, football (1903)

14•STEFFI GRAF, tennis (1969)

13

1987 A new type of football game made its regular-season debut. The Arena Football League, a mini-version of the NFL game, is an indoor league that plays on a 50-yard field with eight players on each side.

1989 The Los Angeles Lakers were trying to win their third straight NBA title. But Laker guards Magic Johnson and Byron Scott were nursing injuries. Without them, the Lakers couldn't keep up with Detroit guards Isiah Thomas and Joe Dumars. The Pistons swept L.A. in four games, winning their first NBA title.

1997 They did it again! The Chicago Bulls defeated the Utah Jazz, 90–86, in Game 6 to win the NBA championship. It is the Bulls' fifth title in seven seasons and their second in a row.

June 13, 1997: Michael Jordan's Chicago Bulls win their fifth NBA championship!

14

1991 Leroy Burrell ran 100 meters in 9.9 seconds to earn the title of "the world's fastest human." Leroy, who set the record at the U.S. championships, in New York City, would hold the record for two months.

1992 The Chicago Bulls beat the Portland Trail Blazers, 97–93, to win their second straight NBA title. For 18 seasons, the NBA did not have a repeat champion. But that changed in a big way. The Los Angeles Lakers won back-to-back titles in 1987 and 1988. Then the Detroit Pistons (1989, 1990) and now the Bulls have done it too!

1994 Fifty-four years of frustration ended in celebration for the New York Rangers. They beat the Vancouver Canucks to claim the Stanley Cup championship. It was their first Cup since 1940!

1902 Nig Clarke set a professional baseball record by smacking eight home runs in eight at-bats. He helped his team, Corsicana, crush Texarkana, 51–3, in a Texas League game.

1938 Today, Johnny Vander Meer of the Cincinnati Reds pitched a no-hitter against the Brooklyn Dodgers. Four days later, on June 19, Johnny will no-hit the Boston Braves. He is the first player to pitch back-to-back no-hitters. Johnny is also the first to throw two no-hitters in one season.

1971 Cheryl White became the first black woman jockey to ride in a race today. The 17-year-old rode a horse named Ace Reward at the Thistledown Race Track, in Cleveland, Ohio.

1989 Four players made holes-in-one on the same hole today! It happened in the second round of the U.S. Open. Doug Weaver, Mark Wiebe, Jerry Pate, and Nick Price all scored an ace on the 167-yard, par 3, sixth hole.

1975 The Los Angeles Lakers traded with the Milwaukee Bucks to get 7'2" center Kareem Abdul-Jabbar. Kareem will help bring five NBA championships to Los Angeles.

1978 Tom Seaver had lost three no-hit bids in the ninth inning in his career. Today, the Cincinnati Red pitcher finally did it: He no-hit the St. Louis Cardinals.

1991 Payne Stewart tied Scott Simpson in the final round of the U.S. Open. Payne will go on to win the Open after a playoff round.

1996 The Chicago Bulls beat the Seattle SuperSonics, 87–75, in Game 6 of the NBA Finals. The victory gave the Bulls their fourth NBA title.

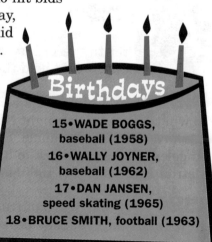

Birthdays

15•WADE BOGGS, baseball (1958)

16•WALLY JOYNER, baseball (1962)

17•DAN JANSEN, speed skating (1965)

18•BRUCE SMITH, football (1963)

17

1962 New York Met "Marvelous" Marv Throneberry connected for a not-so-marvelous triple today. After smacking the ball, Marv zipped around the base paths — but forgot to touch first *and* second base. He was called out!

1978 New York Yankee Ron Guidry set an American League record for lefties when he struck out 18 batters in a game. "Louisiana Lightning" fanned 15 in the first six innings alone!

June 16, 1978: Tom Seaver throws a no-hitter against the St. Louis Cardinals.

1993 Texas Ranger Juan Gonzalez drove in eight runs in today's game against the California Angels. He set a club record for RBIs in a single game! Juan slugged a grand slam and a three-run homer, and he singled home another run.

18

1941 Joe Louis came close to losing his heavyweight title today to Billy Conn, who had been a light heavyweight champ. Billy fought bravely, but Joe finally knocked him out in the 13th round. Joe ended up holding the heavyweight title longer than any other boxer in history — 11 years and 9 months (from June 1937 until June 1949).

1960 Golf great Arnold Palmer was trailing by seven shots when he started the final round of the U.S. Open, in Denver, Colorado. Then he tied a record by shooting a score of 30 for nine holes. Arnie beat Jack Nicklaus by two strokes. He also won the Masters and six other tournaments during the year.

1994 The first ever indoor World Cup soccer match was played today. Eric Wynalda of the United States scored on a 28-yard free kick, giving the U.S. a 1–1 tie with Switzerland.

19

1846 Take me out to Hoboken, New Jersey! The first organized baseball game was played at Elysian Fields, in Hoboken, today. The game lasted four innings. The New York Nine buried the New York Knickerbockers, 23–1. Alexander Cartwright served as umpire. Alexander had written down the first rules of the game. Some people call him "The Father of Baseball."

1984 Jockey Pat Day tied a record with seven wins in eight races at Churchill Downs. Pat is the all-time winningest jockey at the Louisville, Kentucky, track that hosts the Kentucky Derby. At year's end, Pat will be honored with the Eclipse Award as the outstanding jockey of the year.

1990 Golfer Hale Irwin became the oldest man to win the U.S. Open. It wasn't easy: The 45-year-old needed a 45-foot putt on the final hole to force a playoff with Mike Donald. After 18 extra holes, the players were still tied. But Hale got the win in sudden death, sinking an eight-foot birdie putt on the first hole.

20

1968 Jim Hines became the first man to run the 100-meter dash in less than 10 seconds. The American was timed at 9.95 seconds at an AAU (Amateur Athletic Union) track and field championship meet.

1980 The boxing match between Sugar Ray Leonard and Roberto Duran at Montreal's Olympic Stadium was called "The Brawl in Montreal." It ended in a close decision. Sugar Ray suffered his first defeat as a pro and lost his WBC welterweight title to Roberto.

1993 Michael Jordan led the Chicago Bulls to their third straight NBA title. The Bulls became the third team in NBA history to "three-peat." Michael won his third-straight Finals MVP award. Three months later, he will retire from pro basketball.

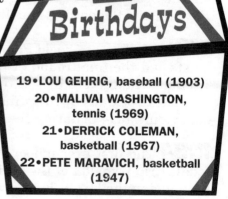

Birthdays

19•LOU GEHRIG, baseball (1903)
20•MALIVAI WASHINGTON, tennis (1969)
21•DERRICK COLEMAN, basketball (1967)
22•PETE MARAVICH, basketball (1947)

JUNE

21

1964 Philadelphia pitcher Jim Bunning gave himself a Father's Day present today: He pitched a perfect game against the New York Mets! It was the first regular-season perfect game (no hits, no walks, no errors) in 42 years. Jim also became the first pitcher to throw a no-hitter in both leagues.

1971 One of Lee Trevino's most thrilling golf victories came at the U.S. Open today. In a playoff, Lee beat Jack Nicklaus by three strokes.

June 22, 1994: America stuns Colombia in World Cup action. The U.S. won, 2–1.

1986 Bo Jackson had won the Heisman Trophy as college football's top player. But today he signed a contract to play *baseball* with the Kansas City Royals. He will later sign to play football with the NFL's Oakland Raiders.

22

1938 Back when Joe Louis and Max Schmeling boxed, the world was on the brink of war. The U.S. and Germany will be enemies in World War II. Joe was American, and Max was German. In 1936, Max had won a boxing war against Joe. Today, Joe got his revenge. He knocked out Max in the first round of their rematch.

1991 The Quebec Nordiques selected Eric Lindros as the top pick in the NHL draft. Eric had impressed scouts with his strength and shooting skill. But Eric refused to play for the Nordiques. After the 1991–92 season, Quebec will send Eric to the Philadelphia Flyers.

1994 Goal! The U.S. soccer team stunned Colombia, 2–1, in World Cup action today. The win sent the Americans to the second round of the World Cup.

JUNE

23

1963 Jimmy Piersall was one of a kind. When he played outfield for the Boston Red Sox, he would bow after making easy catches. He'd also flap his arms like a seal. Today, Jimmy, playing for the New York Mets, hit his 100th career home run. He celebrated by running around the bases backward!

1971 If you want *everything* done right, do everything yourself. In a game against the Cincinnati Reds, Rick Wise did it all. The Philadelphia Phillie right-hander pitched a no-hitter, hit two home runs, and drove in three of the four runs! The Phillies won, 4–0.

1981 A minor-league baseball game that began on April 18 was finally finished. The game, between Pawtucket and Rochester, did not really last 66 days, but it did last 8 hours, 25 minutes. After 32 innings, play was suspended with the score 2–2. When the game resumed today, it took Pawtucket 18 minutes to finish off Rochester.

24

1956 Chris von Slatza broke a women's world record. She swam the 500-yard freestyle in 5 minutes, 52 seconds at a meet in Santa Clara, California. Chris was only 12 years old!

1992 The Orlando Magic and the Charlotte Hornets had the first two picks of the NBA draft. They used those picks to select Shaquille O'Neal of Louisiana State and Alonzo Mourning of Georgetown. During the 1992–93 season, Shaq and Alonzo joined David Robinson, Hakeem Olajuwon, and Patrick Ewing to form one of the best groups of centers ever to play in the NBA at one time.

1995 The New Jersey Devils became Stanley Cup champions today. They clipped the Detroit Red Wings, 5–2. The win completed the Devils four-game sweep of the Stanley Cup Finals. It is the first NHL championship in New Jersey history!

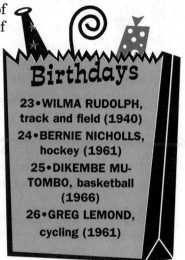

Birthdays

23•WILMA RUDOLPH, track and field (1940)

24•BERNIE NICHOLLS, hockey (1961)

25•DIKEMBE MUTOMBO, basketball (1966)

26•GREG LEMOND, cycling (1961)

JUNE

25

1952 Sugar Ray Robinson, the middleweight champ, could not answer the bell for the 14th round of his fight with light heavyweight champ Joey Maxim. Sugar Ray wilted in the 104-degree heat at Yankee Stadium. It was the only time in 201 bouts that he failed to go the distance.

1968 Bobby Bonds of the San Francisco Giants hit a grand slam home run in his first major league game!

June 24, 1995: The New Jersey Devils win the Stanley Cup!

1977 *Swish!* Ted St. Martin made it into the *Guinness Book of Records* today. He did it by sinking 2,036 free throws in a row.

1981 Sugar Ray Leonard claimed his second professional boxing crown today. The WBC welterweight champ knocked out Ayub Kalule for the WBA junior middleweight title.

26

1944 In the battle of New York City, the Brooklyn Dodgers beat the New York Yankees *and* the New York Giants in the same game! The special game was held to raise money to help the U.S. fight World War II. Each of the three teams took a turn sitting out each inning. The final score of the three-way game was: Dodgers 5, Yankees 1, Giants 0.

1987 Carl Lewis leaped to his 50th straight long-jump win. He also won the 200-meter dash at today's USA/Mobil Outdoor Track and Field Championships, in San Jose, California.

1993 Alexandre Daigle, a center from Canada, was the first player chosen in the NHL draft today. He was selected by the Ottawa Senators. In Alexandre's first season, he placed second on the team in scoring, 28 points behind Alexei Yashin, another rookie.

JUNE

27

1988 Mike Tyson retained his heavyweight boxing crown, giving Michael Spinks a royal beating. Mike scored a first-round knockout in just 91 seconds — four seconds less than it took Jeffrey Osborne to sing the national anthem before the fight! For his work, Mike earned between $18 million and $22 million, or about $220,000 per second.

1992 Decathlon world champion Dan O'Brien was on a world-record pace after the first day of competition at the U.S. Olympic Trials. But he missed his three attempts to clear the minimum height in the pole vault and failed to make the U.S. Olympic Team.

1993 Anthony Young of the New York Mets lost his 24th straight game — a major league record. Anthony will go on to lose 27 straight before finally winning on July 28. In that game, the Mets scored in the bottom of the ninth to beat the Florida Marlins, 5–4.

28

1972 The World Hockey Association (WHA) "stole" one of the NHL's best players today. The Winnipeg Jets signed Chicago Blackhawk great Bobby Hull. The WHA, which has 12 teams, will go out of business in 1979. The Edmonton Oilers, Hartford Whalers, Quebec Nordiques, and Winnipeg Jets are former WHA teams that joined the NHL.

1973 The Black Sports Hall of Fame was formed by *Black Sports* magazine. Thirty-eight athletes were inducted, including football great Jim Brown, tennis star Althea Gibson, and Olympic champs Jessie Owens and Wilma Rudolph.

1991 Barry Larkin of the Cincinnati Reds became the first shortstop to hit five home runs over two consecutive games. Barry will bat over .300 in five seasons, from 1989 to 1993. It will be the first time a shortstop has done that in more than 40 years!

Birthdays

27•VICTOR PETRENKO, figure skating (1969)
28•JOHN ELWAY, football (1960)
29•ROSA MOTA, track and field (1958)
30•MITCH RICHMOND, basketball (1965)

JUNE

29 **1950** In one of the most stunning upsets in World Cup history, the U.S. beat England, 1–0. England had been one of the favorites to win the championship. Most of the Americans were amateurs with other jobs. Two were mailmen and one was a carpenter. The U.S. wouldn't beat England again until June 9, 1993!

1984 Pete Rose of the Cincinnati Reds set a major league record by playing in his 3,309th game. By the time Pete retires, in 1986, he will have played in 3,562 games!

1990 Fernando Valenzuela and Dave Stewart made baseball history by becoming the first pitchers to throw no-hitters on the same day. Fernando pitched his no-hitter for the Los Angeles Dodgers, in a 6–0 win over the St. Louis Cardinals. Dave, pitching for the Oakland A's, beat the Toronto Blue Jays, 5–0.

June 30, 1990: Fernando Valenzuela throws a no-hitter and makes history!

30 **1859** Charles Blondin of France became the first man to cross Niagara Falls on a tightrope. It took five minutes for Charles to complete the 1,100-foot walk across the giant waterfall.

1899 Charles Murphy of New York became the first man to pedal a bicycle as fast as a speeding train. Charles passed a train that was traveling 60 miles per hour!

1994 Oops! Darren Lewis had gone 392 games without making an error. That streak ended today. The San Francisco Giants' centerfielder booted a ground ball in a game against Montreal.

JULY

July 23, 1996: Kerri Strug helps the U.S. Olympic Gymnastics Team win a gold medal.

JULY

1951 Bob Feller of the Cleveland Indians pitched a no-hitter against the Detroit Tigers. It was the third no-hitter of his career! "Rapid Robert" threw blazing fastballs for Cleveland from 1936 to 1956. He missed nearly four seasons while he served in the Navy during World War II. But he will still finish his career with 266 wins.

1990 New York Yankee Andy Hawkins didn't give up a hit, but he still lost today's game, 4–0. The Chicago White Sox scored four runs with two outs in the eighth inning, thanks to two walks and three errors.

1994 Josias and Ravelo Manzanillo became the first brothers in major league baseball history to get saves on the same night. Josias, of the New York Mets, pitched two innings to preserve a 3–1 win over the San Diego Padres. Ravelo, a Pittsburgh Pirate, saved a 6–4 victory against the Cincinnati Reds.

1941 Only 8,682 fans showed up at Yankee Stadium to watch the Yankees play the Boston Red Sox. But they were glad they came. Joe DiMaggio smashed a big home run and broke a major league record by hitting safely in his 44th game in a row! (Joe's streak will end two weeks later at 56 games.)

1988 Steffi Graf defeated Martina Navratilova to win her first Wimbledon title. It brought Martina's Wimbledon winning streak to a halt at eight. In 1995, Steffi will win her sixth Wimbledon championship.

1993 The Philadelphia Phillies and San Diego Padres played for 12 hours today! The first game of their doubleheader started at 4:35 P.M. It ended at 1:03 A.M. (San Diego won, 5–2.) The second game started at 1:28 A.M. Ten innings later, at 4:05 A.M., the Phillies won the game, 6–5.

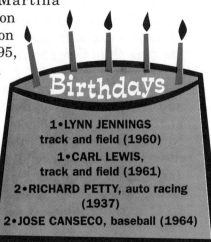

Birthdays

1•LYNN JENNINGS
track and field (1960)

1•CARL LEWIS,
track and field (1961)

2•RICHARD PETTY, auto racing
(1937)

2•JOSE CANSECO, baseball (1964)

3

1954 Babe Didrikson Zaharias had taken time off after having an operation for cancer. Today, she returned to golf and won the U.S. Women's Open for the third time! An all-around athlete, Babe took up golf at the age of 20. She went on to win 31 career titles. She was also one of the founders of the Ladies Professional Golf Association.

1966 Pitchers aren't expected to be good hitters. But Tony Cloninger didn't know that! Tony had the best day at the plate of any pitcher in history in the Atlanta Braves' 17–3 win over the San Francisco Giants. Tony hit two grand slams and drove in nine runs.

1992 Lou Whitaker connected off the Seattle Mariners' Jeff Nelson for the 200th home run of his career. Lou, the Detroit Tiger second baseman, already had 2,000 hits and had played in 2,000 games with the Tigers. He is among Detroit's all-time leaders in doubles, runs scored, and hits.

4

1982 In a meeting of tennis's bad boys at Wimbledon, Jimmy Connors defeated John McEnroe. Jimmy outlasted John in five gritty sets in a match that lasted more than four hours.

1982 What do you get when you combine jogging with juggling? *Joggling*! Ashrita Furman holds the record for the longest time spent running while juggling. She ran a marathon in Salmon, Idaho, and kept three balls in the air for more than three hours!

1993 The world's Number 1 and Number 2 players faced off at this year's Wimbledon final. Number 2 won. Pete Sampras of the U.S. defeated countryman Jim Courier to win his first Wimbledon title and take over the top spot in the rankings. In 1995, Pete will win his third-straight Wimbledon title.

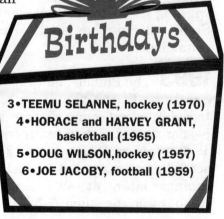

Birthdays

3•TEEMU SELANNE, hockey (1970)

4•HORACE and HARVEY GRANT, basketball (1965)

5•DOUG WILSON,hockey (1957)

6•JOE JACOBY, football (1959)

5

1975 Arthur Ashe became the first African-American player to win the men's singles tennis title at Wimbledon. He defeated Jimmy Connors in four sets.

1992 The U.S. Olympic Basketball Team slam-dunked the last of six opponents to win the Tournament of the Americas. (It is a warm-up tournament for the Olympic Games.) The "Dream Team" won by an average of 51.5 points per game. It beat Venezuela in the final, 127–80.

July 3, 1954: Babe Didrikson Zaharias returns to golf and wins the U.S. Women's Open for the third time!

1992 Andre Agassi of the U.S. and Goran Ivanisevic of Croatia battled through five sets in the men's final at Wimbledon. Andre, who had lost three Grand Slam finals, won the championship.

6

1983 Comiskey Park, in Chicago, is the site of baseball's first All-Star Game. Today, it hosted the 50th anniversary of the Midsummer Classic. Fred Lynn of the California Angels hit the first grand slam in All-Star history, powering the American League to its first victory in 12 years.

1985 Tennis players Martina Navratilova and Pam Shriver had not lost a doubles match since April 24, 1983 — a record that spanned 109 straight matches! Their streak was finally broken in the Wimbledon final by Kathy Jordan and Liz Smylie.

1994 Leroy Burrell regained the title of world's fastest man. (He had lost it to Carl Lewis three years earlier.) At a meet in Lausanne, Switzerland, Leroy zipped through the 100-meter dash in 9.85 seconds, snipping .01 of a second off the world record.

JULY

7

1985 Boris Becker crushed Kevin Curren to become the youngest Wimbledon champion ever. The 17-year-old Boris fired 21 aces in the final and became the first unseeded man to capture the Wimbledon trophy. "Boom Boom" Becker will win again in 1986 and 1989.

1986 Jackie Joyner-Kersee wowed the fans with a record-setting performance at the Goodwill Games, in Moscow, the Soviet Union (now Russia). The world heptathlon champ finished the seven-event, two-day competition with 7,148 points, breaking the world record by 202 points.

1990 Martina Navratilova used her powerful serve-and-volley game to capture a record ninth Wimbledon title. She won her nine Wimbledon crowns in a span of 13 years, including six in a row.

8

1889 Before boxers wore gloves, they brawled with bare hands. The last bare-knuckle bout took place today. John L. Sullivan successfully defended his heavyweight title against Jake Kilrain. The fight lasted 75 rounds.

1912 New York Giant pitcher Rube Marquard gave up six runs in six innings in a 6–2 loss to the Chicago Cubs. That loss ended Rube's major league-record streak of 19 straight wins in one season. No other pitcher has come close to breaking that record.

1980 J.R. Richard, the fireballing right-hander of the Houston Astros, was the National League's starting pitcher in today's All-Star Game. Twenty-two days later, he will suffer a stroke that will end his career.

1994 Alex Rodriguez of the Seattle Mariners made his first major league start. The 18-year-old was the youngest player to reach the major leagues since Jose Rijo joined the New York Yankees in 1984.

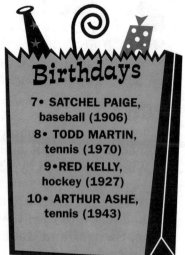

Birthdays

7• SATCHEL PAIGE, baseball (1906)

8• TODD MARTIN, tennis (1970)

9• RED KELLY, hockey (1927)

10• ARTHUR ASHE, tennis (1943)

9

1977 Golfer Tom Watson set a record for the lowest 72-hole score (268) in the history of the British Open championship. It was Tom's second Open win. He will take the title again in 1982 and 1983.

1984 The U.S. Olympic Basketball Team stunned the NBA All-Stars, 97–82, in a game at the Indianapolis Hoosier Dome. The Olympic team had a few future NBA all-stars on board. The gold medal-winning team included Michael Jordan, Chris Mullin, Patrick Ewing, and Sam Perkins.

July 7, 1986: Heptathlon champ Jackie Joyner-Kersee soars to a world record.

1994 Brazil beat the Netherlands, 3–2, in a quarterfinal match of the World Cup. All five goals came in a 30-minute span in the second half. A 30-yard free kick in the 81st minute decided the soccer tournament's most dramatic game.

1934 The American League won the second annual All-Star Game. New York Giant Carl Hubbell struck out five future Hall of Famers in a row: Babe Ruth, Lou Gehrig, Jimmie Foxx, Al Simmons, and Joe Cronin!

1994 Golfer Kim Williams finished 10th in the Jamie Farr Toledo Classic. It was just days after she was shot in the neck. (Kim was in an Ohio drugstore when she was hit by a stray bullet.)

1994 Al Unser, Junior, won the Grand Prix of Cleveland today. His average speed of 138 miles per hour over 85 laps set a track record. By year's end, "Little Al" will have won 8 of his 16 races.

JULY

11

1985 Nolan Ryan of the Houston Astros fanned Danny Heep of the New York Mets to become the first pitcher in major league history to strike out 4,000 batters. Nolan, who will finish his career with a record 5,714 strikeouts, will lead the league in strikeouts 11 times!

1989 Bo Jackson of the Kansas City Royals received the Most Valuable Player trophy as he led the American League to its second consecutive All-Star Game victory. Bo smashed the second pitch he saw over the centerfield fence at Anaheim Stadium.

1993 French auto racer Alain Prost is the all-time leader in Formula One victories. Today, he won his 50th career race, at the British Grand Prix, in Silverstone, England. In the Portuguese Grand Prix, on September 26, Alain will finish in second place, clinching his fourth world driving title.

12

1979 Disco Demolition Night at Comiskey Park was not a sound idea. Tickets were sold for 98 cents to all fans who brought a disco record to burn between games of a doubleheader between the Chicago White Sox and Detroit Tigers. When the fans refused to leave the field after the fire, the Sox had to forfeit the second game.

1992 Atlanta Brave shortstop Jeff Blauser blasted three home runs in one game! He lifted the Braves to a 7–4 win over the Chicago Cubs. Jeff's power performance was the only three-homer game of the season.

1994 The National League All-Stars edged the American League All-Stars, 8–7, in extra innings in Pittsburgh. The victory was the first for the National League since 1987. Atlanta Brave Fred McGriff, whose ninth-inning home run tied the game, was named the MVP.

Birthdays

11•ROD STRICKLAND, basketball (1966)

12•KRISTI YAMAGUCHI, figure skating (1971)

13•SPUD WEBB, basketball (1963)

14•LEE ELDER, golf (1934)

JULY

13

1934 Babe Ruth became the first player ever to hit 700 home runs in a career. The New York Yankee slugger sent a towering homer over the rightfield wall — and onto the street!

1991 Four arms are better than one. Four Baltimore Oriole pitchers — Bob Milacki, Mike Flanagan, Mark Williamson, and Gregg Olson — combined to no-hit the Oakland Athletics, 2–0.

July 13, 1934: New York Yankee slugger Babe Ruth smashes his 700th career home run.

1994 Whenever Italy needed a goal in 1994 World Cup action, Roberto Baggio would give it his best shot. He scored the winning goal late in today's soccer match between Italy and Bulgaria. Roberto had also kicked in the game winner in the previous two World Cup rounds!

14

1951 For the first time, television viewers watched a sporting event in color. It was a horse race — the Molly Pitcher Handicap — and it was shown live from New Jersey.

1992 They don't call them All-Stars for nothing. The American Leaguers set an All-Star Game record with 19 hits today. They trounced the National Leaguers, 13–6. (Ken Griffey, Junior, of the Seattle Mariners was the game's MVP.)

1993 Baseball is known as "America's national pastime." Maybe it should be known as "Cuba's national pastime," too! Why? The Cubans have one of the best amateur baseball teams in the world. Today, the team from Cuba beat the squad from the United States at the World University Games in Buffalo, New York.

1990 Golfer Betsy King wasn't having a great day. She was 11 shots behind in the U.S. Women's Open, and the action was delayed by rain. When the skies cleared, Betsy stormed back. She won her second-straight Open title! (Betsy will qualify for the LPGA Hall of Fame on June 25, 1995.)

1993 Baltimore's Cal Ripken, Junior, hit his 278th home run as a shortstop today — the most ever hit by a major leaguer at that position. Cal's blast broke Ernie Banks's record of 277 homers.

1994 One month after guiding the New York Rangers to the Stanley Cup, coach Mike Keenan announced that he was leaving the team. Two days later, he will agree to become the coach and general manager of the St. Louis Blues.

1909 The Washington Senators and Detroit Tigers played the longest scoreless game in American League history. The game was called after 18 innings with the score tied, 0–0!

1950 There were more than 200,000 people in the stands to watch Brazil face Uruguay in the World Cup, in Rio de Janiero, Brazil. It was the biggest crowd ever to watch a soccer game.

1988 Florence Griffith Joyner smashed the 100-meter world record with a time of 10.49 seconds. FloJo's dazzling performance came in the quarterfinal heat at the U.S. Olympic Trials, in Indianapolis. She went on to capture Olympic gold medals in the 100-meter dash, the 200-meter dash (setting a world record), and the 400-meter relay.

1989 After winning three auto races in a row, Emerson Fittipaldi's streak was cut short by driver Bobby Rahal. Bobby zoomed past Emerson in the Marlboro Grand Prix.

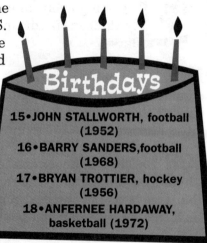

Birthdays

15 • JOHN STALLWORTH, football (1952)

16 • BARRY SANDERS, football (1968)

17 • BRYAN TROTTIER, hockey (1956)

18 • ANFERNEE HARDAWAY, basketball (1972)

17

1941 The Cleveland Indians jolted Joe DiMaggio by holding him hitless in today's game. The New York Yankee had hit safely in 56 consecutive games. It's a major league record that may never be broken.

1987 Don Mattingly of the New York Yankees hit a very big home run today. Not only did the shot help the Yankees win the game, but it also earned Don a place in the history books. He became the first American Leaguer to hit at least one homer in seven straight games!

1994 Nick Price of Zimbabwe came from behind to win golf's British Open. He did it by making a 50-foot eagle putt on the 17th hole. Nick, who was the 1993 Player of the Year, would finish 1994 as the top money winner in men's golf.

July 16, 1988: Florence Griffith-Joyner blazes through the 100-meters in record time.

18

1908 Believe it or not, the tug-of-war was once an Olympic event. During the first round of the competition at the Olympics, a team from Great Britain beat the U.S. in a matter of seconds. The Americans complained that the English used illegal boots with spikes to dig into the ground. After the judges rejected their claims, the U.S. team pulled out of the competition. Britain will win all three medals!

1987 Don Mattingly did it again. He hit another home run, extending his streak to eight games. That tied a major league record!

1994 At the end of the World Cup Final soccer game, the score was tied, 0–0. The world champion would be crowned after a tie-breaking shoot-out. Brazil outshot Italy, 3–2 to win the title.

JULY

19

1877 The first Wimbledon tennis tournament finals were held in England today. Only 200 fans came out to see it. (Spencer Gore won the men's competition. Maud Watson was Wimbledon's first women's singles champ.)

1911 Minor league outfielder Walter Carlisle didn't need any help today. Walter, who was a former circus acrobat, completed an unassisted triple play. No other outfielder had done that before. And none has done it since!

1994 When umpires heard that Albert Belle of the Cleveland Indians might have corked his bat, they took the bat away (it's against the rules to use a bat containing cork). Then the bat disappeared! When it finally turned up, it was found to have cork in it. Albert got a seven-game suspension as punishment.

20

1859 What a bargain! For the first time, fans paid to watch a baseball game. Each ticket cost 50 cents. Admission prices have gone up a little bit since then! The fans saw New York outslug Brooklyn, 22–18.

1924 U.S. swimmer Sybil Bauer swamped the competition in the women's 100-meter backstroke at the Olympics today. She won in 1 minute, 23.2 seconds — an Olympic record. At the time of her win, Sybil held every swimming record for women. She never lost a race in her career.

1973 Wilbur Wood of the Chicago White Sox started both games of a doubleheader. No one else has done that since! (Wilbur and the Sox lost both games to the New York Yankees.)

1976 Hank Aaron cracked the 755th — and last — home run of his amazing career today. "Hammerin' Hank" averaged 33 homers and 100 RBIs per season over his 22-year career.

Birthdays

19•ILIE NATASE, tennis (1946)
20•CHUCK DALY, basketball (1946)
21•ANITA NALL, swimming (1976)
22•MICHAEL SPINKS,
boxing (1956)

JULY

21 **1952** Shot putter Parry O'Brien of the U.S., hurled the shot put 57'1½" to set an Olympic record and collect the gold medal. Parry used a new shot-putting style that quickly became very popular.

1956 Pittsburgh's Roberto Clemente hit a three-run home run **July 22, 1976: Nadia Comaneci _(shown with trick photography)_ scores the first 10 in Olympic history!** that helped the Pirates come from behind and notch a 4–3 win over the Cincinnati Reds. Cincinnati Red pitcher Brooks Lawrence took the loss, ending his 13-game winning streak.

1987 Lady's Secret, a 4-year-old filly, won at Monmouth Park race track to become the top money winner among female horses in racing history.

22 **1976** Fourteen-year-old Nadia Comaneci became the first gymnast to score a perfect 10 at the Olympics. Nadia earned the score in the uneven parallel bars competition. By the end of the Games, she had received seven perfect 10's and won three gold medals. (Nadia also won a silver and a bronze.)

1976 Swimmer Kornelia Ender set the world record in the 100-meter butterfly at the Olympics in Montreal (Canada). Thirty minutes later, she set the world record in the 200-meter freestyle! Kornelia, age 18, won four gold medals and one silver at the Games.

1984 At the Summer Olympics, in Atlanta, Georgia, weightlifter Naim Suleymanoglu set a world record for the 141-pound weight class. He lifted 738 pounds to win his third Olympic gold medal. Naim is nicknamed Pocket Hercules.

JULY

23 **1989** American Greg LeMond had chased France's Lauren Fignon for 23 days and more than 2,000 miles in cycling's Tour de France. Going into the final 15 miles of the race, Greg was trailing. He gave it all he had and finished eight seconds ahead of Lauren to grab his second Tour win.

1991 What did Pittsburgh Pirate Gary Redus, Kansas City Royal Todd Benzinger, Baltimore Oriole Randy Milligan, and Seattle Mariner Ken Griffey, Junior, have in common tonight? They all hit grand-slam homers! The four-slam day tied a major league record.

1996 In the most dramatic moment of the Summer Olympics, held in Atlanta, Georgia, gymnast Kerri Strug took her second vault and landed on her badly sprained ankle. She took a few painful hops, then fell to the floor in tears. The vault earned 9.712 points and helped the U.S. Women's Gymnastics Team win its first gold medal in the team competition.

24 **1983** George Brett found himself in a sticky situation today. In the ninth inning of a game between the Kansas City Royals and New York Yankees, he hit a home run to give the Royals a 5–4 lead. But George's bat had a lot of pine tar on it. (Players use pine tar to keep their hands from slipping.) Baseball rules allow players' bats to have 18 inches of tar, but the umpires said George had more than that. His homer was not allowed and the Yanks won the game. (The decision was later overruled.)

1987 Boris Becker of West Germany defeated John McEnroe of the United States in a Davis Cup match that lasted 6 hours 38 minutes. (The Davis Cup is a tennis tournament between men's teams from different countries.)

1994 Spain's Miguel Indurain won the Tour de France. It was the fourth-straight time he had won the major cycling event.

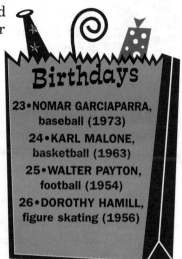

Birthdays

23•NOMAR GARCIAPARRA, baseball (1973)

24•KARL MALONE, basketball (1963)

25•WALTER PAYTON, football (1954)

26•DOROTHY HAMILL, figure skating (1956)

JULY

25 **1939** Thanks to pitcher Atley Donald, the New York Yankees were able to beat the St. Louis Browns, 5–1. Not only did Atley get his 12th-straight victory, but he set an American League record for a rookie starting pitcher.

1976 In his first international meet, U.S. track and field star Edwin Moses set a world record in the 400-meter hurdles at the Olympics. Edwin's performance earned him a gold medal.

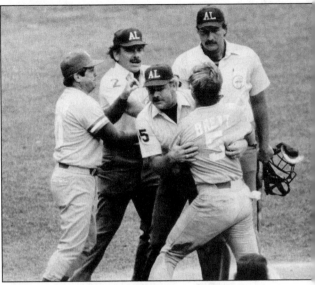

July 24, 1983: George Brett loses a homer when umpires say his bat is illegal.

1994 Kansas City's Bob Hamelin hit a three-run homer in the 12th inning today! The Royals won the game against Chicago and started a winning streak that would last 14 games. At the season's end, Bob was named Rookie of the Year.

26 **1859** Ivy League schools battled in the first college rowing regatta, held in Worcester, Massachusetts. Harvard, Yale, and Brown Universities faced off, and Harvard sailed to victory.

1954 A minor league team from Welch, West Virginia, set a baseball record today. The team made triple plays in back-to-back innings. It's the only time in professional baseball history in which the same team made a triple play two innings in a row.

1981 Pat Bradley and Beth Daniel had been co-leaders in the U.S. Women's Open since the sixth hole of the final round. On the 15th hole, Pat sank a 70-foot birdie putt for a one-stroke lead. It was enough to give her the tournament win. Pat's final score of 66 and total score of 279 were tournament records.

27

1984 Pete Rose shattered Ty Cobb's record for most singles in a career. Playing for the Montreal Expos, Pete hit his 3,053rd single against the Philadelphia Phillies. But he didn't stop there. He went on to break Ty's record for most career hits, with 4,256.

1987 During an exhibition game between the Atlanta Braves and the New York Yankees, Pam Postema made baseball history. She became the first woman ever to work as a plate umpire in a major league game.

1992 After failing to make the 1988 Olympic team, United States swimmer Pablo Morales took a three-year break from swimming to study law. Today, Pablo dove back in and captured the Olympic gold medal in the 100-meter butterfly.

1993 Put your arms over your head and reach up as high as you can. Javier Sotomayor of Cuba can still jump over you. At a meet in Salamanca, Spain, Javier broke his own world high-jump record. He cleared the bar at 8' ½".

28

1993 Seattle Mariner slugger Ken Griffey, Junior, homered in his eighth-straight game today. The blast tied a major league record. (Dale Long of Pittsburgh did it in 1956 and Don Mattingly of the Yankees repeated the feat in 1987.)

1994 Texas Ranger hurler Kenny Rogers pitched a perfect game. It was the first ever by a left-hander in the American League. Ranger centerfielder Rusty Greer saved the perfect game with a diving catch in the ninth inning.

1994 After a strong World Cup performance, Alexi Lalas signed with the team in Padova, Italy. He is the first U.S. player to compete in Italy's Series A league.

Birthdays

27•PEGGY FLEMING, figure skating (1948)
28•VIDA BLUE, baseball (1949)
29•GEORGE DIXON, boxing (1870)
30•CHRIS MULLIN, basketball (1963)

 **1978** Penny Dean of California dove into the English Channel today and started swimming. She made it from England to France in just 7 hours, 40 minutes. It was a new record for the Channel swim!

1983 Steve Garvey had set an N.L. record for consecutive games played on April 6. The Los Angeles Dodger first baseman's streak had climbed to 1,207 games since. But it ended today — Steve dislocated his thumb in a play at the plate.

July 30, 1992: Gymnast Shannon Miller flies into second place at the Olympics.

1994 In his 354th minor league at-bat, Michael Jordan hit his first home run. After retiring from basketball, Michael played left-field for the Birmingham Barons. The Barons are a Class AA team in the Chicago White Sox farm system.

1976 At the Olympics, in Montreal, Canada, Bruce Jenner became an instant hero. The American won the gold medal in the 10-event decathlon and set a world record for most points in the event.

1992 Shannon Miller won the silver medal in the all-around gymnastics competition at the Summer Olympics. The American gymnast was edged out for the gold by 0.025 of a point by the Unified Team's Tatiana Goutsou. (The Unified Team was made up of athletes from nations of the former Soviet Union.)

1995 Philadelphia Phillie third baseman Mike Schmidt was inducted into the Baseball Hall of Fame. Mike spent his entire 18-year career with the Phillies, from 1972 to 1989. He won the National League's Most Valuable Player award three times! In 1980, Mike led the Phillies to their first ever World Series championship.

JULY

1954 Milwaukee Brave first baseman Joe Adock set a major league record by hitting for 18 total bases in five at-bats. He hit four home runs (for 16 bases) and a double (two bases). The Braves beat the Dodgers, 15–7.

1984 The Chinese were expected to win most of the medals in men's gymnastics at the Olympics. But the athletes from the U.S. surprised everyone by winning seven. They even took the gold in the team competition!

1994 San Francisco Giant third baseman Matt Williams hit his 40th home run of the season. It was a National League record for homers hit before August. Matt was on a pace to break Roger Maris's single-season record of 61. But, on August 12, a baseball strike will end the season and Matt's streak.

1994 Sergei Bubka of Ukraine set his 35th world record in the pole vault. He cleared 20' 1¾". (About how high is that? Picture five kids standing on one another's shoulders!) Sergei set his first record 10 years before. He has added nearly a foot to that record since then.

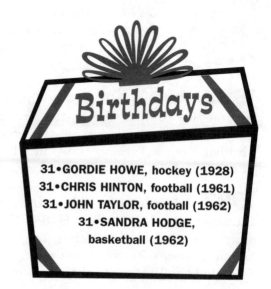

Birthdays

31•GORDIE HOWE, hockey (1928)
31•CHRIS HINTON, football (1961)
31•JOHN TAYLOR, football (1962)
31•SANDRA HODGE,
basketball (1962)

AUGUST

August 8, 1984:
Diver Greg Louganis
wins his first Olym-
pic gold medal.

1

1982 Greg Louganis earned a 10 (a perfect score) from all seven judges at a diving competition in Central America. He is one of just two male divers ever to get a perfect score on a dive from every judge.

1992 U.S. track-and-field star Gail Devers won the gold medal in the 100-meter sprint at the Olympics. Just 16 months earlier, Gail had been suffering from Graves' disease, which weakens muscles, blurs vision, and causes weight loss. Gail's treatments caused her feet to swell so badly she could barely walk. By winning an Olympic gold, Gail had made one of the greatest comebacks in sports history.

1996 It was a great day for the U.S. at the Summer Olympics, for two reasons: In track, sprinter Michael Johnson shattered his six-week-old record in the 200 meters with a time of 19.32 seconds. The victory earned Michael his second gold medal of the Games. Also, in the first Olympic women's soccer final, the U.S. beat China 2–1 to win the gold medal. Tiffeny Milbrett scored the game-winner in the second half.

2

1938 If you saw a bright yellow ball zooming through the air, you might think you were at a tennis match. Not today! The Brooklyn Dodgers and St. Louis Cardinals tested a yellow baseball in a game. They hoped it would be easier for batters to see. It wasn't.

1984 Olympic wrestler Jeff Blatnick of the U.S. is a true fighter. First, Jeff won a two-year battle with cancer. Then, on this day, he won the gold medal in the super heavyweight division at the 1984 Olympics.

1992 Jackie Joyner-Kersee won her second straight gold medal in the Olympic heptathlon. The heptathlon is a two-day, seven-event competition in women's track and field. Jackie later won a bronze medal in the long jump. In three Olympics, she has won three gold medals, a silver, and a bronze.

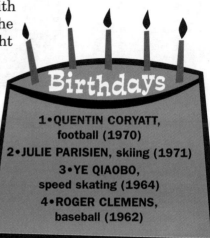

Birthdays

1•QUENTIN CORYATT, football (1970)

2•JULIE PARISIEN, skiing (1971)

3•YE QIAOBO, speed skating (1964)

4•ROGER CLEMENS, baseball (1962)

3

1960 In sports, it's common for players to get traded. But the Cleveland Indians and Detroit Tigers made history today by trading *managers!* It had never been done before.

August 3, 1984: Mary Lou Retton lands a gold medal with her perfect scores.

1984 Mary Lou Retton struck gold in Los Angeles, California. The 16-year-old gymnast did it by getting perfect scores in the floor exercise and vault at the Olympics. She won the gold medal in the all-around competition.

1989 The Cincinnati Reds had the Houston Astros seeing red today. The Big Red Machine churned out 14 runs in the bottom of the first! In the half inning, which lasted 38 minutes, the Reds blasted 16 hits. That's a major league record for a first inning. Cincinnati crushed Houston, 18–1.

4

1984 Carl Lewis won the first gold medal of his Olympic career today, in the 100-meter dash. Before the end of the Games, the U.S. track and field star would add three more medals — in the 200-meter run, long jump, and 4 x 100 meter relay. Carl became the second person in history to win four gold medals in track and field at one Olympics. (Jesse Owens did it first. He had been Carl's boyhood idol.)

1985 Two future Hall of Famers reached baseball milestones on this day. Rod Carew of the California Angels collected the 3,000th hit of his career, and Tom Seaver of the Chicago White Sox won his 300th game.

1993 Tony Gwynn of the San Diego Padres made a career-high six hits in one game. Tony tied the major league record shared by Willie Keeler, Ty Cobb, and Stan Musial.

5

1936 Jesse Owens of the U.S. ran the 200-meter sprint in record time — 20.7 seconds — to win a gold medal at the Summer Olympics, in Berlin, Germany. It was one of the four gold medals Jesse will win at that Olympics.

1984 Joan Benoit of the United States won the first women's Olympic marathon ever held. But Joan almost didn't make it to the starting line. Seventeen days before the U.S. Olympic Trials (tryouts), Joan had had knee surgery.

1996 The Chicago Bulls re-signed forward Dennis Rodman to a contract for the 1996–97 season. The one-year deal is worth slightly less than $10 million. Dennis rewards the Bulls by winning his sixth straight rebounding title. No other player in NBA history has won that many rebounding titles in a row.

6

1926 Gertrude Ederle became the first woman to swim the English Channel. The Channel is a 21-mile body of water that separates England from France. Gertrude made the swim in record time — 14 hours, 31 minutes.

1972 Hank Aaron of the Atlanta Braves broke Babe Ruth's record for most home runs hit with one team today. Hank belted the 660th and 661st home runs of his career, against the Cincinnati Reds.

1992 Kevin Young of the United States set the only world record at the 1992 Summer Olympics. He won the gold medal in the 400-meter hurdles in 46.78 seconds. He broke Edwin Moses' nine-year-old record.

1992 San Diego Padre teammates Gary Sheffield and Fred McGriff hit back-to-back homers in back-to-back innings against the Houston Astros.

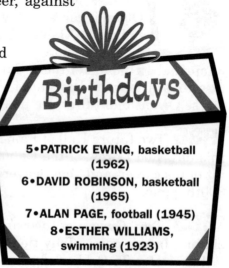

Birthdays

5•PATRICK EWING, basketball (1962)

6•DAVID ROBINSON, basketball (1965)

7•ALAN PAGE, football (1945)

8•ESTHER WILLIAMS, swimming (1923)

7 **1952** At age 46, Satchel Paige of the St. Louis Browns became the oldest man ever to throw a complete game shutout. Satchel pitched 12 scoreless innings to defeat the Detroit Tigers, 1–0.

1992 Jennifer Capriati of the U.S. was the underdog in the tennis final at the Olympic Games. She had never won a major tournament. Her opponent, Steffi Graf, had won 11. Steffi won the first set, but Jennifer powered back to win the match and the gold medal.

August 8, 1992: The first U.S. Dream Team wins the Olympic gold medal in basketball.

1992 Shaquille O'Neal, the NBA's top draft pick, signed a seven-year contract with the Orlando Magic. During his rookie season, Shaq will average a team-best 23 points and 14 rebounds per game. Orlando will finish with the best record in its history.

8 **1976** The Chicago White Sox really showed their socks today. They became the first major league baseball team to wear shorts as part of their uniform. After today, they will never wear shorts again!

1984 Greg Louganis won the springboard diving competition at the Summer Olympics. Four days later, Greg will win the platform diving competition, too. Greg will become the first male diver since 1928 to win both events. He also will set world records in both.

1992 The U.S. Olympic Basketball "Dream Team" won the gold medal at the Summer Games. It was the first U.S. Olympic basketball team to include NBA players. The Dream Team was as good as advertised: It won by an average of 44 points per game!

9

1939 A scoring streak that has never been topped began today. New York Yankee third baseman Red Rolfe scored a run in a game to start an 18-game scoring streak. Red scored 30 runs during those 18 games! No one else has ever scored at least one run in that many games in a row.

1988 Wayne Gretzky was traded from the Edmonton Oilers to the Los Angeles Kings. "The Great One" will go on to become the NHL's all-time leading scorer.

1988 The Chicago Cubs played the first official night game at Wrigley Field, their home park. Wrigley was the last major league baseball stadium to install lights.

10

1944 Red Barrett of the Boston Braves needed 58 pitches — an average of 6.4 pitches per inning — to shut out the Cincinnati Reds, 2–0. The teams combined to set a record for fewest pitches thrown in a nine-inning game.

1974 Jorge Lebron, a 14-year-old shortstop from Puerto Rico, became the youngest person ever to play pro baseball. Jorge played for a Philadelphia Phillie farm club. Today's game had to start early so that it would be over by Jorge's bedtime! Jorge played in three games, then he returned to Puerto Rico to attend junior high school.

1980 Baseball's Pete Rose rapped his 3,631st career base hit, breaking Stan Musial's record for most hits in the National League in a career.

1984 The Olympic 3,000-meter race was a long-awaited showdown between two great runners — Mary Decker of the U.S. and Zola Budd of South Africa (running for Great Britain). Midway through the race, the two runners bumped into each other. Mary was injured and fell to the ground. Zola finished the race, but the winner was Marcica Puica of Romania.

Birthdays

9•DEION SANDERS, football (1967)

10•ROCKY COLAVITO, baseball (1933)

11•CRAIG EHLO, basketball (1961)

12•PETE SAMPRAS, tennis (1971)

11

1973 Jean Balukas, just 14 years old, won her second U.S. Open Pocket Billiards women's championship. The year before, she had become one of the youngest champions in the history of the sport.

1984 An event called rhythmic gymnastics was introduced at the Summer Olympics. In rhythmic gymnastics, female athletes do floor exercises using ribbons, balls, Indian clubs, and hoops. Synchronized swimming was also added to the Olympics in 1984.

August 10, 1984: Mary Decker collides with Zola Budd and drops out of the 3,000-meter race.

1991 Just in the nick of time! Golfer John Daly got to play in the PGA Championship as a last-minute replacement for another golfer, who had dropped out. John had to drive all night to make it to the tournament on time to start play. It was worth the trip . . . he won the tournament.

12

1975 John Walker of New Zealand became the first person to run a mile in less than 3 minutes, 50 seconds. John was clocked in a world-record time of 3 minutes, 49.4 seconds. He ran his final lap faster than any of his first three laps. That Walker sure could run!

1986 Don Baylor of the Boston Red Sox was hit by a pitch for the 25th time in the season, setting a record. Don, who is now the manager of the Colorado Rockies, also holds the American League career record for most times hit by a pitch, 267 times.

1994 Hey, where did everyone go? One strike and everyone was out. Major league baseball players went on strike, bringing the season to a grinding halt.

AUGUST

1919 The great race horse Man O' War had only lost one race in his career. Today, he was upset by a horse actually named Upset. (The word *upset* would be a part of sports vocabulary from that day on.)

1987 Jackie Joyner-Kersee became the first American woman to hold the world long-jump record. She leaped 24' 5½" at the Pan American Games to tie a record first set by Heike Dreschler of Germany in 1986. That record was later broken, but Jackie increased the American record to 24' 7" in 1994.

1989 Golfer Payne Stewart shot a final-round 67 to overtake 10 other players and win the PGA Championship. Payne played the last nine holes in an amazing 31 shots, to win his first major title.

1936 Basketball on a tennis court? That's where the first Olympic basketball championship game was played today. Rain had soaked the clay courts, which made for a muddy game. The U.S. trudged through the low-scoring contest, defeating Canada, 19–8, and winning the gold medal.

1976 New Jersey's Giants Stadium was crammed with a record 77,691 fans. It was the quarter-final playoff game of the North American Soccer League. The New York Cosmos beat the Fort Lauderdale Strikers, 8–3.

1986 Baseball's Pete Rose collected the final hit of his career. It was his 4,256th hit — more than any other player in history. Pete will retire on August 17, 1986, after 23 years in the major leagues.

1987 Oakland A's slugger Mark McGwire hit his 39th homer of the season, setting a rookie record. He finished the season with 49 homers to lead the American League. Mark's hitting earned him the Rookie of the Year award.

Birthdays

13•MIDORI ITO, figure skating (1969)
14•MAGIC JOHNSON, basketball (1959)
15•GENE UPSHAW, football (1945)
16•KRISZTINA EGERSZEGI, swimming (1974)

15

1941 The Washington Senators lost a game today because of an error — by the grounds crew! Washington was down three runs when it started to rain. The crew took a long time to cover the field. Umpires ruled that the crew did it on purpose, hoping the game would get rained out.

1990 He's got the magic touch! First baseman Mark McGwire of the Oakland A's hit his 30th home run of the season — a

August 14, 1987 *and* August 15, 1990: Mark McGwire slugs his way into the record books.

grand slam! He became the first player in baseball history to hit 30 homers in each of his first four seasons.

1993 San Francisco Giants Barry Bonds and Matt Williams hit back-to-back home runs twice today. The four homers came in a game against the Cubs at Wrigley Field, in Chicago.

16

1921 This was news! Suzanne Lenglen lost a tennis match today. After trailing in the second round of the U.S. Open, Suzanne had to stop playing because she was ill. She would never lose another match in her seven-year career!

1954 *Sports Illustrated* magazine published its first issue. It was the first weekly magazine about sports in the country. Milwaukee Brave slugger Eddie Mathews was on the first cover.

1976 The St. Louis Cardinals defeated the San Diego Chargers in a pre-season football game played in Tokyo, Japan. More than 30,000 fans watched the first NFL game played outside North America.

AUGUST

17

1917 Gertrude Ederle was 12 years old, but she wasn't too young to set a world record in swimming. Gertrude zipped through the women's 880-yard freestyle event in 13 minutes 19 seconds at a meet in Indianapolis, Indiana. She is the youngest person ever to set a world record.

1933 New York Yankee great Lou Gehrig played in his 1,308th game in a row, setting a major league record. But Lou was just getting warmed up. He would play in 2,130 straight games before sitting one out in 1939.

1987 Today, Steffi Graf of Germany became the top-ranked woman player in tennis. (Martina Navratilova had held the number 1 ranking for five straight years.) Steffi held on to the Number 1 spot until March 10, 1991.

1990 Carlton Fisk of the Chicago White Sox smacked his 328th homer. That blast helped him pass Johnny Bench to become the all-time home run leader among catchers.

18

1989 *You're out of here!* Dallas Green became the 17th manager to be fired by New York Yankee owner George Steinbrenner. Bucky Dent took over as the new skipper of the Bronx Bombers.

1992 Basketball star Larry Bird called it quits after 13 seasons with the Boston Celtics. Larry had led Boston to three NBA titles and earned three straight league MVP awards. Many considered him the greatest forward in NBA history.

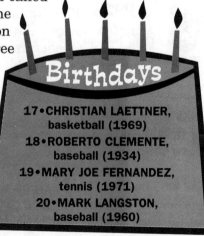

Birthdays

17•CHRISTIAN LAETTNER,
basketball (1969)
18•ROBERTO CLEMENTE,
baseball (1934)
19•MARY JOE FERNANDEZ,
tennis (1971)
20•MARK LANGSTON,
baseball (1960)

1993 At the Greater Harrisburg Open, bowler Walter Ray Williams, Junior, was on a roll. He bowled four perfect games in the tournament — a new PBA record. (In a perfect game, a bowler rolls 12 strikes in a row for a score of 300.)

19 **1917** New York Giants manager John McGraw and Cincinnati Red manager Christy Mathewson were both arrested today. They were guilty of committing the same crime: playing baseball on a Sunday. In those days, many states had laws against playing sports on Sundays.

August 18, 1992: After 13 seasons, basketball great Larry Bird says he's done.

1951 Eddie Gaedel became the smallest man ever to play professional baseball. Eddie, who was 3' 7" tall and weighed 65 pounds, pinch-hit for the St. Louis Browns. Wearing uniform number ⅛, Eddie walked on four pitches. It was his only turn at bat in the major leagues.

1992 Bret Boone started at second base for the Seattle Mariners, becoming the first third-generation player in major league history. Bret's dad, Bob Boone, and grandfather, Ray Boone, were successful major leaguers.

20 **1974** Nolan Ryan threw the fastest pitch ever clocked in a major league baseball game today. The California Angel right-hander unleashed one fastball that was timed at 100.9 miles per hour! Nolan struck out 19 Detroit Tigers in the game.

1991 Miami Dolphin quarterback Dan Marino became the highest paid player in NFL history today. Dan agreed to a five-year contract worth $25 million — an average of $5 million per season.

1994 The famous Travers Stakes horse race matched the two best 3-year-old thoroughbreds of the year, Holy Bull and Tabasco Cat. Holy Bull thundered to a clear victory, finishing 17 lengths ahead of Tabasco Cat, who came in third.

21 **1902** That's a no-no! Pitcher Joe "Iron Man" McGinnity was booted out of the National League after stepping on an umpire's toes, spitting in his face, and punching him. Joe's fans begged the National League to give him another chance . . . and the league took him back.

1908 In a dangerous stunt, a member of the Washington Senators baseball team went to the top of the Washington Monument, in Washington, D.C., and dropped balls to Senator catcher Gabby Street. The balls were thrown from a window 555 feet up. Gabby actually caught one! Scientists figured that when the ball reached him, it had a force of 200 to 300 pounds.

1982 Relief pitcher Rollie Fingers of the Milwaukee Brewers notched his 300th career save — a major league record. Rollie closed out a 3–2 Brewer victory over the Seattle Mariners.

22 **1917** Pittsburgh Pirate Carson Bigbee made 11 trips to the plate in a 22-inning game today. His 11 at-bats tied a major league record. The Pirates had gone into extra innings three game in a row. They set a National League record by playing 59 innings in four games!

1951 In Berlin, West Germany (now Germany), 72,000 fans came to Olympic Stadium to watch the Harlem Globetrotters perform. It was the largest crowd ever to attend a basketball game.

1971 A volleyball team became the second U.S. team to travel to Cuba since Communist leader Fidel Castro took power in 1959. Cuba beat the U.S. and earned a spot in the 1972 Olympics.

1989 Nolan Ryan became the first pitcher to strike out 5,000 batters in a career. Number 5,000 was Rickey Henderson, who whiffed on a 3–2 pitch in the fifth inning.

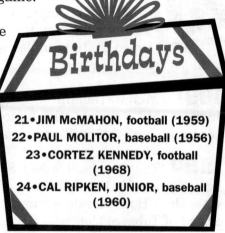

Birthdays

21•JIM McMAHON, football (1959)
22•PAUL MOLITOR, baseball (1956)
23•CORTEZ KENNEDY, football (1968)
24•CAL RIPKEN, JUNIOR, baseball (1960)

23 **1989** The team from San Pedro, California, won the Little League World Series, with the help of Victoria Brucker. Victoria scored three runs in the game to help San Pedro defeat the team from Tampa, Florida, 12–5. Victoria was the first girl ever to play for a U.S. team in the Little League World Series.

August 24, 1963: John Pennel uses a fiber-glass pole to break his pole-vaulting record.

1992 Both pitchers threw no-hitters in today's game between the Clearwater Phillies and the Winter Haven Red Sox, two minor league clubs. Winter Haven built a run with two walks and two sacrifice bunts. It was all they needed to win this Class A game.

1992 Oakland A's reliever Dennis Eckersley preserved a 7–3 victory over the Baltimore Orioles to register his 40th save of the season. That made Dennis the first pitcher in history to save 40 games in four different seasons! During that time, the A's won an amazing 52 straight games in which Dennis appeared.

24 **1963** He's up! John Pennel pole-vaulted to a height of 17' 3⅛" — breaking his own record. John, who was the first man to clear 17 feet, did it using a fiberglass pole. (Before John, most vaulters used wooden poles.)

1975 He's out . . . at last! Montreal Expo catcher Gary Carter threw out Los Angeles Dodger Davey Lopes as he tried to steal second base. Davey had stolen 38 bases in a row without being caught.

1985 *Bonk!* Today, Don Baylor of the New York Yankees tied an American League career record by getting hit by a pitch for the 189th time in his career.

1985 Dwight Gooden started his own 20–20 club today. Dwight, who was 20 years old, won his 20th game. The New York Met was the youngest pitcher ever to win that many games in a season.

1990 Detroit Tiger slugger Cecil Fielder became the first Tiger ever to crack a home run over Tiger Stadium's leftfield roof. Cecil joined Harmon Killebrew (1962) and Frank Howard (1968) as the only batters to send a ball out of this ballpark.

1991 American sprinters swept the medals in the 100-meter dash at the World Track and Field Championships, in Tokyo, Japan. It was the fastest race in the history of the event, with six of the eight competitors finishing under 10 seconds flat! Carl Lewis won in the world-record time of 9.86 seconds. Leroy Burrell finished second in 9.88. Dennis Mitchell was third at 9.91.

1939 For the first time ever, baseball fans got to watch a game on television. The Cincinnati Reds defeated the Brooklyn Dodgers in the history-making game. But there were not many fans tuned in to the broadcast — there were only about 400 television sets in all of New York State at the time!

1987 Paul Molitor's 39-game hitting streak was on the line. As he stood on deck in the 10th inning, Paul was 0 for 4. He would never get a fifth chance to get a hit. The Milwaukee Brewers scored the winning run against the Cleveland Indians, ending the game and Paul's streak.

1989 A team from Trumbull, Connecticut, won the Little League World Series. The victory was just the second for an American team in the last 23 years! (Teams from Taiwan had won 13 World Series during that time.) Led by 12-year-old pitcher Chris Drury, the U.S triumphed over Taiwan, 5–2.

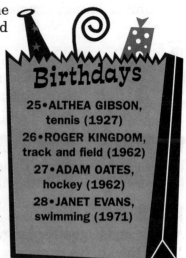

Birthdays

25•ALTHEA GIBSON,
tennis (1927)

26•ROGER KINGDOM,
track and field (1962)

27•ADAM OATES,
hockey (1962)

28•JANET EVANS,
swimming (1971)

AUGUST

 **27**

1982 Rickey Henderson of the Oakland A's stole a very big base today — his 119th of the season! That set a major league record for most stolen bases in a season. (Lou Brock had held the record with 118.)

1989 There he goes again! A month after winning the Tour de France with a late charge, cyclist Greg LeMond pulled off another come-from-behind victory at the World Cycling Championships, also in France. Greg became the fifth man in history to win both races in the same year!

1994 Dominique Dawes swept all five events at the U.S. gymnastics championships. Dominique won the all-around, the balance beam, the uneven bars, the floor exercise, and the vault. She was the first to sweep the events since 1969.

August 25, 1991: Carl Lewis sets a world record in the 100-meters.

28

1977 Pelé was the world's greatest soccer player, and today he retired. But first, he helped the New York Cosmos win the North American Soccer League (NASL) Championship over the Seattle Sounders. More than 35,000 fans showed up to watch the superstar play his final NASL game. New York defeated Seattle, 2–1. Pelé scored 1,281 goals in his career — about a goal per game.

1978 Donald Vesco of Loma Linda, California, set the world record for the fastest speed on a motorcycle — 318.66 miles per hour. He rode a special twin-engined, streamlined bike called "Lightning Bolt" at the Bonneville Salt Flats, in Utah.

1994 Golfer Tiger Woods, age 18, won his first U.S. Amateur championship. On the final day, he rallied from six shots behind the leader. Tiger is the first African-American to win the U.S. Amateur. He is also the youngest winner in the history of the event.

29

1974 High school hotshot Moses Malone was selected by the Utah Stars in the American Basketball Association draft. The 6' 10" center became the first basketball player ever to go straight from high school into a pro league. (During the 1995 NBA draft, Kevin Garnett was selected out of high school by the Minnesota Timberwolves.) Moses will be still going strong at age 40, playing for the San Antonio Spurs.

1992 Charlie Leibrandt struck out the 1,000th batter of his career. The Atlanta Brave pitcher wanted a souvenir of the milestone, so he rolled the ball into the dugout for safekeeping. But no one had called timeout and a base runner was allowed to advance! Charlie's play was ruled a throwing error. Sorry, Charlie.

1993 Jockey Laffit Pincay, Junior, rode El Toreo to victory in the seventh race at Del Mar racetrack. It was his 8,000th win. Laffit is the top career money winner, with more than $17 million in purses.

30

1987 Canadian Ben Johnson raced to the title of "The World's Fastest Human" today. He set a 100-meter record of 9.83 seconds at the world championships in Rome, Italy. In 1989, Ben will be stripped of the record after it is discovered that he used the illegal drugs called steroids.

1991 Mike Powell of the U.S. broke an amazing record at the World Track and Field Championships. Mike long-jumped 29' 4½" to shatter the world record. The old record had lasted 23 years. It was set by Bob Beamon of the United States at the 1968 Olympic Games.

1994 Pittsburgh Penguin Mario Lemieux had suffered with back problems and Hodgkin's disease. Today, he announced that he would sit out the 1994–95 season. (Mario will return for the 1995–96 season.)

Birthdays

29•EDDIE MURRAY, football (1956)

30•TED WILLIAMS, baseball (1918)

31•EDWIN MOSES, track and field (1955)

31•FRANK ROBINSON, baseball (1935)

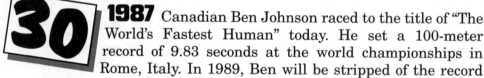

31 **1972** You're late! Americans Rey Robinson and Ed Hart were disqualified from the Olympic 100-meter event when they didn't show up for the race. The U.S. coach had given them the wrong time!

1990 The family that plays together, stays together. Ken Griffey, Senior, age 40, and Ken Griffey, Junior, age 20, became the first father and son to play on the same major league team. Two weeks later, the Griffeys hit back-to-back home runs!

August 31, 1990: Ken Griffey, Senior *(left)*, and Ken, Junior become teammates!

1992 The Oakland A's traded Jose Canseco — the first player to hit 40 home runs and steal 40 bases in the same season — to the Texas Rangers for three players. Jose was in the on-deck circle when he was called back to the dugout and told about the trade.

SEPTEMBER

Sports Illustrated

SEPTEMBER 4, 1972   60 CENTS

OLYMPIAN
MARK
SPITZ

September 4, 1972: Swimmer Mark Spitz wins his seventh Olympic gold medal.

1 **1946** Golfer Patty Berg won the first U.S. Women's Open. Patty did much to build the Ladies Professional Golf Association (LPGA). She was the LPGA's first president, and her 57 tour victories rank third on the all-time list. She entered the LPGA Hall of Fame in 1951.

1972 Shane Gould swam to her third Olympic gold medal and third Olympic record. The 15-year-old Australian finished the 200-meter freestyle in 2 minutes, 3.56 seconds.

1991 Running back Thurman Thomas became the first player in Buffalo Bill history to record 100 yards rushing and 100 yards pass receiving in the same game. He rushed for 165 yards and caught eight passes for 103 yards in the Bills' 35–31 win over Miami.

2 **1907** Ty Cobb stole second base, third base, and home in the same game! Ty was a fierce base runner. Some say that he even sharpened his spikes so that infielders would fear his slides. Ouch!

1960 Wilma Rudolph beat the odds by winning the gold medal in the 100 meters at the Olympics. When Wilma was a kid, she had a serious disease called polio. She had to wear a brace on her left leg until she was 12. By age 20, Wilma was an Olympic champion. She also won gold medals in the 200 meters and the 4x100-meter relay.

1990 It was a long time coming, but Dave Stieb of the Toronto Blue Jays finally pitched a no-hitter. Dave had entered the ninth inning with a no-hitter in four other games, only to give up a hit each time.

1992 Bobby Fischer played his first public game of chess in 20 years. Bobby, one of the world's best chess masters, beat Boris Spassky for the championship. Bobby has not defended his title since then.

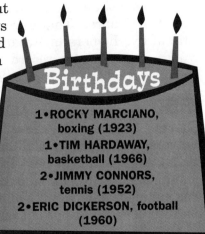

Birthdays

1•ROCKY MARCIANO, boxing (1923)

1•TIM HARDAWAY, basketball (1966)

2•JIMMY CONNORS, tennis (1952)

2•ERIC DICKERSON, football (1960)

3

1895 The very first professional football game was played by two teams from Pennsylvania. The team from Latrobe beat the squad from Jeanette, 12–0. It was a professional game only because Latrobe quarterback John Brallier was paid $10 to cover his expenses.

1911 William A. Larned won his fifth-straight singles competition at the U.S. Open Tennis Championships. It was his seventh win overall. William will become the second player to win seven men's titles at the U.S. Open. (Richard D. Sears was the first.)

1977 Baseball crowned a new home-run king — Sadaharu Oh. Sadaharu was the greatest player in the history of professional baseball in Japan. He slugged his 756th homer today. That's one more than Hank Aaron hit in his major league career. Sadaharu will retire in 1980 with 868 home runs.

4

1972 Mark Spitz of the United States swam on the winning 4x100-meter medley relay team, collecting his seventh gold medal at the Summer Olympics, in Munich, West Germany. Mark set world records in all but one of the seven events he won. His record of winning seven gold medals at one Olympics still stands today. In all, Mark won 11 Olympic medals in his swimming career!

1985 New York Met catcher Gary Carter hit two home runs in a game against the San Diego Padres. That gave Gary a total of five homers in two days — tying a major league record. (The Mets pounded the Padres, 9–2.)

1993 Welcome back, Miller! Cheryl Miller, who led the University of Southern California to NCAA women's basketball championships in 1983 and 1984, was named the new women's basketball coach at her old school.

Birthdays

3 • MARK WITHERSPOON, track and field (1963)

4 • MIKE PIAZZA, baseball (1968)

5 • DENNIS SCOTT, basketball (1968)

6 • KEVIN WILLIS, basketball (1962)

SEPTEMBER

5 **1918** United States soldiers were in Europe, fighting in World War I. During the seventh-inning stretch of this day's World Series game between the Red Sox and the Cubs, a band played "The Star Spangled Banner" and the whole crowd sang along. The national anthem had never been played at a sporting event before.

1979 Anne Meyers made history by becoming the first woman to sign a con- **September 4, 1985: New York Met Gary** tract to play for an NBA **Carter hits his fifth homer in two days!** team. The former star at the University of California at Los Angeles played one week in training camp with the Indiana Pacers before she was cut from the team.

1994 In the San Francisco 49ers' 44–14 win over the Los Angeles Raiders, Jerry Rice scored three touchdowns. The last of those TDs, a 38-yard catch late in the fourth quarter, was Jerry's 127th career touchdown. That was an NFL record.

6 **1976** Chris Evert won her second-straight U.S. Open tennis championship. The triumph capped her three-year run as the top woman player in the world.

1988 Thomas Gregory, an 11-year-old English boy, swam across the English Channel today. Thomas was the youngest person ever to make the 21-mile swim between England and France.

1995 When Cal Ripken, Junior, walked onto the field tonight, he stepped into history. The Baltimore Oriole shortstop was playing in his 2,131st straight game! He broke Lou Gehrig's record for consecutive games played. (Cal hit a home run to celebrate.)

7

1970 Jockey Bill Shoemaker set a horse-racing record by winning his 6,033rd race. By the time he retired, in 1990, Bill had ridden more than 8,800 winners during his 41-year career.

1991 Quarterback Ty Detmer of Brigham Young University became the NCAA career passing leader with 11,606 yards, in BYU's 27–23 loss to UCLA. Ty will end his varsity career with 15,031 passing yards, for an average of 326.7 yards per game.

1993 St. Louis Cardinal Mark Whiten had the best one-game offensive performance in major league baseball history. Mark hit *four* home runs and drove in 12 runs against the Cincinnati Reds. Mark was only the second player to have 12 RBIs in one game.

1997 It was a battle of teenagers in the U.S. Open women's singles final. Top-ranked Martina Hingis, age 16, defeated unseeded Venus Williams, age 17. The 6–0, 6–4 win gave Martina her third Grand Slam title of the year. She raised her 1997 record to 63–2.

8

1965 Bert Campaneris of the Kansas City A's became the first player in modern baseball history to play all nine defensive positions in one game. Bert, usually a shortstop, played a different position in each inning!

1969 Australian Rod Laver won the U.S. Open to capture the Grand Slam of tennis. (He won Wimbledon and the Australian, French, and U.S. Opens in the same year.) Rod is the only player to win the Grand Slam twice. He first did it in 1962.

1990 Gabriela Sabatini won her first Grand Slam tennis title today. She upset superstar Steffi Graf in the U.S. Open final. Gabriela was seeded Number 5 in the tournament and became the lowest seed to win in 22 years. She also became the first woman from Argentina to win a Grand Slam tennis tournament.

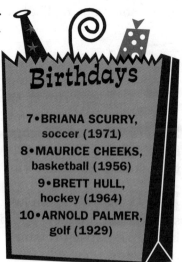

Birthdays

7•BRIANA SCURRY, soccer (1971)

8•MAURICE CHEEKS, basketball (1956)

9•BRETT HULL, hockey (1964)

10•ARNOLD PALMER, golf (1929)

9

1972 Happiness turned to sadness for the United States Olympic Basketball Team. Just as the squad began to celebrate its victory over the Soviet Union, officials ordered three seconds be put back on the clock. The Russians scored and won the gold medal by 1 point.

1990 Nineteen-year-old Pete Sampras became the youngest man ever to win the U.S. Open. Pete, who was seeded Number 12 in the tournament, had aces up his sleeve. He blasted 100 serves that his opponents couldn't return!

September 10, 1988: Steffi Graf wins the U.S. Open and the Grand Slam of tennis.

1992 With a line-drive single to rightfield, Robin Yount of the Milwaukee Brewers reached the 3,000-hit mark. Robin, who has won two Most Valuable Player awards (one at shortstop, the other in centerfield), was the 17th major leaguer to collect 3,000 hits.

10

1974 Lou Brock was one of baseball's greatest base stealers. On this day, he swiped his 105th base of the season, breaking the big-league record set by Maury Wills. By the time he retired, Lou had stolen 938 bases.

1988 Steffi Graf won the U.S. Open to become the fifth player to win the Grand Slam of tennis. Steffi went on to win the gold medal at the Summer Olympics later in the year.

1992 Atlanta Brave baseball player Deion Sanders signed a one-year contract to play football with the Atlanta Falcons. Three days later, Deion will return a kickoff 99 yards for a touchdown!

1974 The St. Louis Cardinals defeated the New York Mets, 4–3, in the longest completed game in major league baseball history. The game went 25 innings and took more than seven hours to complete.

1985 With his hometown crowd cheering, Pete Rose of the Cincinnati Reds lined a single that broke Ty Cobb's record for career hits. Pete's hit was the 4,192nd of his career. He finished his career with 4,256 hits and is still Number 1 on the all-time hits list.

1994 The game between the Kansas City Chiefs and the San Francisco 49ers featured a matchup of former teammates, Joe Montana and Steve Young. When both quarterbacks played for the 49ers, Joe was the teacher, Steve the student. In this day's game, Joe threw two touchdown passes, as the Chiefs won, 24–17.

1994 Andre Agassi completed an amazing run to the U.S. Open championship. Andre entered the Open unseeded and with five seeded players in his way. He defeated them all, including Michael Stich in the straight-set final, 6–1, 7–6, 7–5.

1976 Minnie Minoso of the Chicago White Sox became the oldest player in major league history ever to get a base hit. When Minnie smacked his record-setting single today, he was 53 years old.

1987 Paul Lynch of Great Britain did a lot of push-ups in 24 hours — 32,573, to be exact. That's about 23 push-ups every minute! (It was also a world record.)

1992 When Monica Seles arrived at the U.S. Open, she caught a cold. But even sick, Monica was better than anyone else. After defeating six other players, she beat Arantxa Sanchez Vicario in the final.

Birthdays

11•TOM LANDRY, football (1924)

12•JESSE OWENS, track and field (1913)

13•AJ KITT, skiing (1968)

14•TIM WALLACH, baseball (1957)

13

1980 The East Carolina University football team set an embarrassing record today. The Pirates fumbled five times on five straight possessions in one quarter! Southwestern Louisiana converted on four of the fumbles for scores, and won, 27–21.

September 11, 1985: Pete Rose passes Ty Cobb to become baseball's all-time hit leader.

1989 Jockey Pat Day knows the way to the winner's circle at Arlington Park, in Chicago. He made it there eight times today! Pat rode the winner in eight out of nine races — the best one-day winning percentage for a jockey. In Pat's only loss, he came in second.

1992 "Put me in, Coach, I'm ready to play!" That may be what punters Chris Mohr of the Buffalo Bills and Joe Prokop of the San Francisco 49ers were singing as the Bills outscored the 49ers, 34–31. The game featured 1,086 yards of offense and for the first time in NFL history, no punts.

14

1986 Los Angeles Raider running back Marcus Allen extended to 11 his NFL record for most consecutive 100-yard rushing games. He rushed for 100 yards in the last nine games of 1985, and the first two games of this season.

1990 The Griffeys — 20-year-old Ken junior and 40-year-old Ken senior — hit back-to-back home runs today as teammates on the Seattle Mariners. It was a baseball first!

1991 Fifteen-year-old Kim Zmeskal, of Houston, Texas, became the first American woman ever to win the all-around gold medal at the World Gymnastics Championships.

15

1938 Lloyd and Paul Waner, both with the Pittsburgh Pirates, slugged back-to-back home runs in a game against the New York Giants. That's the only time brothers have hit successive homers in a major league game.

1963 The outfield was filled with Alous in today's game between the San Francisco Giants and the Pittsburgh Pirates. The Alou brothers — Felipe, Matty, and Jesus — all played together in the Giant outfield for one inning. (The Giants won, 13–5.)

1969 Steve Carlton of the St. Louis Cardinals pitched the game of his life, and lost. Steve struck out 19 batters (a record), but New York Met outfielder Ron Swoboda connected for a pair of two-run homers. The Mets cut the Cards, 4–3.

1990 Bobby Thigpen of the Chicago White Sox preserved a 7–4 win over the Boston Red Sox, and became the first pitcher to record 50 saves in a season. Bobby went on to extend his record to 57 saves. He only blew eight chances in 77 appearances.

16

1975 Rennie Stennett wasn't known for his hitting . . . until today! The Pittsburgh Pirate tied a big-league record for hits in a nine-inning game. He got seven hits in Pittsburgh's 22–0 romp over the Chicago Cubs.

1989 It was a classic college football battle between Number 1-ranked Notre Dame and Number 2-ranked Michigan. Notre Dame's outstanding receiver and kick returner, Raghib "Rocket" Ismail, returned two kick-offs for touchdowns. The Fighting Irish beat the Wolverines, 24–19.

1993 Dave Winfield of the Minnesota Twins became the 19th major leaguer to join the 3,000-hit club. He did it with a ninth-inning single off Oakland reliever Dennis Eckersley.

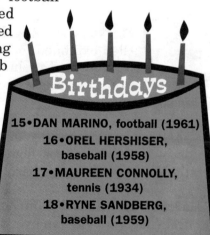

Birthdays

15•DAN MARINO, football (1961)

16•OREL HERSHISER, baseball (1958)

17•MAUREEN CONNOLLY, tennis (1934)

18•RYNE SANDBERG, baseball (1959)

17

1920 The American Professional Football Association was formed today. Ten teams, including the Decatur Staleys, Canton Bulldogs, and Dayton Triangles, each paid $100 to enter the league. Four more teams will join in November. Two years later the league will change its name to the National Football League (NFL).

1984 Reggie Jackson of the California Angels hit the 500th home run of his career. He became the 13th player in major league history to hit 500 homers. Reggie hit his first big-league homer 17 years earlier, also on this day.

September 17, 1989: Randall Cunningham passes for 447 yards and five TDs.

1989 Philadelphia Eagle quarterback Randall Cunningham completed 34 passes for 447 yards and five touchdowns in today's game. He lifted his team from a 20–0 hole to a 42–37 win over the Washington Redskins.

18

1968 Copycat! The day after San Francisco Giant Gaylord Perry pitched a no-hitter against St. Louis, Cardinal pitcher Ray Washburn no-hit the Giants. The back-to-back no-hitters were a baseball first.

1984 Joe W. Kittinger of Orlando, Florida, crossed the Atlantic Ocean in a 10-story hot-air balloon. And he did it all by himself!

1988 Seattle Seahawk wide receiver Steve Largent broke the NFL record for receiving yardage in a career. When Steve caught a 19-yard pass in today's game against San Diego, his career total hit 12,148 yards. (He broke the record by two yards.)

1943 It's about time! The Detroit Lions kicked off the season with a win. They defeated the Chicago Cardinals, 35–17. It was the first time the Lions had won since November 30, 1941!

1988 Swimmer Janet Evans gave the United States its first gold medal at the Summer Olympics, in Seoul, South Korea. The high school senior won the 400-meter individual medley. Janet would also win gold in the 400-meter and 800-meter freestyles and add a world record to her collection during the Games. (She holds three world records.)

1993 San Diego Charger placekicker John Carney set the NFL record for consecutive field goals, at 29. He hit six of them in today's game against Houston. John kicked the game-winner from 27 yards with three seconds left!

1931 Evar Swanson, a former football and baseball star, set a speed record for running around the bases. In a special exhibition, he started at home and circled a major league-sized infield in 13.3 seconds!

1973 When tennis player Bobby Riggs boasted that he could beat any woman at tennis, Billie Jean King decided to prove him wrong. She played Bobby in a match that was shown on national TV and beat him in three straight sets.

1992 Philadelphia Phillie second baseman Mickey Morandini turned in the first unassisted triple play in the National League since 1927. Pittsburgh's Jeff King hit a line drive up the middle, which Mickey caught for the first out. Mickey then stepped on second base to double-up Andy Van Slyke, and tagged out Barry Bonds, who was standing near second. It was the ninth unassisted triple play in major league history.

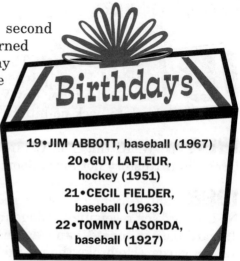

Birthdays

19•JIM ABBOTT, baseball (1967)
20•GUY LAFLEUR, hockey (1951)
21•CECIL FIELDER, baseball (1963)
22•TOMMY LASORDA, baseball (1927)

1934 Dizzy and Paul Dean of the St. Louis Cardinals were dazzling in a doubleheader against the Brooklyn Dodgers. In the opener, Dizzy pitched a three-hit shutout. In the nightcap, Paul pitched a no-hitter.

1968 Texas coach Darrell Royal showed off the new Wishbone offense. The Wishbone is a T formation with a twist. Halfbacks line up farther from the line of scrimmage than the fullback, making the backfield look like a wishbone. The team will win the national title in 1969 using the Wishbone!

September 19, 1988: Swimmer Janet Evans wins her first Olympic gold medal.

1982 NFL players walked off the job for the first time in the league's history. The strike will last until November 17, 1982.

1911 Boston Brave pitcher Denton "Cy" Young won the 511th — and final— game of his career today. The Braves defeated Pittsburgh, 1–0. Cy's 511 career victories is a record that may never be broken.

1927 Gene Tunney, the heavyweight boxing champion of the world, was knocked down during a bout with Jack Dempsey. But instead of moving to a neutral corner, Jack stood over Gene. The ref did not start the 10-count until Jack moved. Before the ref finished counting, Gene got up. He went on to win the fight in a decision and keep his title. The fight is known as "the long-count fight."

1990 Howard Griffith of the University of Illinois set an NCAA record by scoring eight touchdowns in a game! Howard, who gained 208 yards in the 56–21 victory, didn't even play in the fourth quarter!

23 **1908** The New York Giants thought they had won the game that clinched the National League pennant. But, thanks to Fred Merkle, the Chicago Cubs won the battle *and* the war. Fred was the Giant base runner on first when a teammate's hit against the Cubs drove in what should have been the game-winning run. The Giants started to celebrate. But Fred forgot to tag second base after the hit. He was out! The ump called the game a tie, and the Giants and Cubs had to play again the next day. The Cubs won the game and the pennant.

1988 Jose Canseco of the Oakland A's stole two bases in a game against the Milwaukee Brewers to become the first baseball player to hit more than 40 home runs (he hit 42) and steal 40 bases in the same season.

1992 Goalie Manon Rheaume of the Canadian national women's hockey team became the first woman to play in an NHL game. Manon appeared in an exhibition game for the Tampa Bay Lightning.

24 **1967** Placekicker Jim Bakken of the St. Louis Cardinals set an NFL record by kicking seven field goals in a game against the Pittsburgh Steelers. The Cardinals won the game, 28–14.

1972 In a game against the Green Bay Packers, Oakland Raider defensive back Jack Tatum scooped up a fumble in his own end zone. Then he returned it 104 yards for a touchdown!

1988 Jackie Joyner-Kersee won a gold medal and set the world record in the heptathlon (a seven-event competition) with 7,291 points at the Summer Olympic Games, in Seoul, South Korea. Jackie would also win the gold medal in the long jump at the Games, soaring to a distance of 24' 3¼." It was an Olympic record.

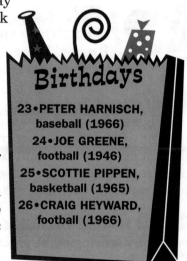

Birthdays

23•PETER HARNISCH, baseball (1966)

24•JOE GREENE, football (1946)

25•SCOTTIE PIPPEN, basketball (1965)

26•CRAIG HEYWARD, football (1966)

25

1965 At the age of 59, Satchel Paige pitched three innings for the Kansas City A's. He became the oldest player ever to play in a major league game. His earned run average for the day was perfect — Satchel didn't give up a single run.

1986 Great Scott! Houston Astro righthander Mike Scott pitched a no-hitter as the Astros clinched the National League West division title. Never had a baseball title been clinched on a no-hitter. Mike, who used a split-fingered fastball to win 18 games, led the league in strikeouts and ERA for the season.

September 23, 1992: Manon Rheaume is the **first woman ever to play in the NHL.**

1989 Boston Red Sox third baseman Wade Boggs went four-for-five against the New York Yankees and became the first American Leaguer to get 200 hits in seven straight seasons. It's no surprise that Wade won five A.L. batting titles during that time, too.

26

1981 Houston Astro pitcher Nolan Ryan no-hit the Los Angeles Dodgers, 5–0. The no-hitter was the record-setting fifth of Nolan's career. (On September 23, 1973, Nolan, then with the California Angels, had set another record — he struck out his 383rd batter of the season.)

1981 University of North Carolina running back Kelvin Bryant scored four touchdowns in leading the Tar Heels to a 56–14 win over Boston College. The performance gave Kelvin 15 touchdowns in three games, an NCAA record.

1983 *Australia II*, skippered by John Bertrand, sailed to victory in the America's Cup. It was the first time in 132 years that a crew from a foreign country won the America's Cup trophy.

1930 Golfer Bobby Jones defeated Gene Homans in the title match at the U.S. Amateur championship. The victory was Bobby's fourth major tournament victory that season, making him the only golfer to achieve a Grand Slam.

1960 In his final major league at-bat, Ted Williams hit a home run! The Boston Red Sox slugger ended his career with 521 homers and a .344 batting average. He won six batting titles and led the American League in homers and RBIs four times.

1988 Greg Louganis made a near-perfect dive at the Summer Olympics, in Seoul, South Korea, to win the 10-meter platform event and his second gold medal. Greg is the first male diver to win the springboard and platform events in back-to-back Olympics.

1941 Entering the last day of the season, Boston's Ted Williams was batting an even .400. His manager offered to let him sit out the games to protect his average, but Ted wanted to play. He cracked six hits in eight at-bats to finish at .406. Ted is the last player to bat .400 or more in a season.

1955 Jackie Robinson stole home in Game 1 of the World Series between the Brooklyn Dodgers and New York Yankees. The Dodgers fell one run short in this game, but went on to win their first World Series championship.

1988 Pitcher Orel Hershiser of the Los Angeles Dodgers hurled his 59th straight scoreless inning. That broke a 20-year-old major league record set by Dodger Don Drysdale.

1997 In the final game of the season, slugger Mark McGwire of the St. Louis Cardinals ripped his 58th home run of the year. Only Babe Ruth (59 in 1921 and 60 in 1927) and Roger Maris (61 in 1961) have hit more home runs in one season.

Birthdays

27 • MIKE SCHMIDT, baseball (1949)

28 • STEVE LARGENT, football (1954)

29 • KEN NORTON, JUNIOR, football (1966)

30 • MARTINA HINGIS, tennis (1980)

1954 New York Giant Willie Mays made an amazing over-the-shoulder catch in today's game. The catch robbed Cleveland's Vic Wertz of a hit and saved the Giants' victory in Game 1 of the World Series. The blast would have been a home run in most ballparks, but with Willie on patrol in the sprawling Polo Grounds, it was just a 460-foot out.

1987 Ask Don Mattingly to describe his season in one word and he might say "Grand." Why? The Yankee slugger hit his sixth grand slam of the season today! It's a major league record.

1988 At the Olympics, in Seoul, South Korea, Florence Griffith Joyner won a gold medal and set a world record in the 200 meters. FloJo also won gold medals in the 100 meters and the 4x100-meter relay. (Her sister-in-law, Jackie Joyner-Kersee, won two gold medals at the Seoul Games, too.)

September 28, 1997: It's home run number 58 for Mark McGwire!

1927 Babe Ruth broke his own record by hitting his 60th home run of the season. Babe, who finished the season with a .356 batting average, led the American League in home runs 10 times in 15 seasons.

1992 On the 20th anniversary of the day Pittsburgh Pirate great Roberto Clemente got his 3,000th hit, George Brett of the Kansas City Royals became the 18th major leaguer to get 3,000 hits.

1997 Tim Raines, Derek Jeter, and Paul O'Neill of the New York Yankees slugged back-to-back-to-back home runs against the Cleveland Indians in Game 1 of the division playoffs. The Yankees were the first team to hit three straight homers in a post-season game.

OCTOBER

October 18, 1977:
Reggie Jackson hits
three home runs in a
World Series game.

1 **1932** Babe Ruth hit his last home run in World Series play today. It was one of the most famous moments in sports history! As he stepped up to the plate, he pointed to centerfield as if to say "that's where I'm going to hit a home run." And he did! No one knows for sure if Babe really meant to call the shot — he wouldn't say.

1961 In the last game of the year, Roger Maris set a record for hitting the most home runs in a season — 61. The New York Yankee outfielder sent the ball over the rightfield fence at Yankee Stadium. No one has broken Roger's record of 61 in '61.

1977 Good-bye, Pelé. More than 75,000 fans came to Giants Stadium, in New Jersey, to say farewell to the world's greatest soccer player. Pelé retired after today's special exhibition game.

2 **1968** Bob Gibson of the St. Louis Cardinals fanned 17 Detroit Tigers in today's World Series opener. He set a record for most strikeouts in one game. The Cards beat the Tigers, 4–0, but Detroit took the series.

1978 New York Yankee fans gained a new hero today — Bucky Dent. In a special one-game playoff for the A.L. East division title, Bucky hit a three-run blast over the "Green Monster" (the leftfield wall in Boston's Fenway Park). The Yankees won, 5–4.

1993 John Olerud of the Toronto Blue Jays won the American League batting title with a .363 average. His teammates Paul Molitor and Roberto Alomar finished second and third in the batting race. It was the first time this century that a league's top three hitters were teammates.

1994 Don Shula's Miami Dolphins defeated David Shula's Cincinnati Bengals, 23–7, in the first father-and-son coaching duel in NFL history.

Birthdays

1•GRETE WAITZ,
track and field (1953)
1•MARK McGWIRE,
baseball (1963)
2•MARK RYPIEN,
football (1962)
2•JANA NOVOTNA,
tennis (1968)

OCTOBER

3

1951 The New York Giants and Brooklyn Dodgers were playing the game that would decide the N.L. pennant winner. In the bottom of the ninth inning, the Dodgers led 4–2. Bobby Thompson of the Giants stepped up to the plate with two men on. He hit a 315-foot shot over the left-field wall! The Giants won the game and the pennant. The homer is still known as "the shot heard round the world."

1973 Plans for a new pro football league were announced today. The World Football League (WFL) was formed to compete against the NFL. The league lasted two years.

1989 Art Shell became the first black head coach in NFL history. Art, a Hall of Fame offensive lineman who played for the Oakland Raiders for 15 seasons, was named to lead his old team.

4

1955 After losing the first two games of the World Series, the Brooklyn Dodgers bounced back to win it all in seven games. No team had ever made that kind of comeback in World Series play before. Johnny Podres pitched a shutout in the seventh game to beat the New York Yankees.

1963 Led by Sandy Koufax, the Los Angeles Dodgers swept the New York Yankees in the World Series. It was the first time the Yanks had gone winless in a Series since 1922.

1992 Texas Ranger Juan Gonzalez hit his 43rd home run in the last game of the season. Juan edged the Oakland A's Mark McGwire by one homer to win the American League home run title.

1994 Martina Hingis of the Czech Republic was just four days past her 14th birthday when she joined the women's pro tennis tour. Martina beat 45th-ranked Patty Fendick, 6–4, 6–3, at the European Indoors championships, in Zurich, Switzerland.

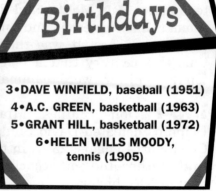

Birthdays

3•DAVE WINFIELD, baseball (1951)
4•A.C. GREEN, basketball (1963)
5•GRANT HILL, basketball (1972)
6•HELEN WILLS MOODY, tennis (1905)

5 **1974** David Kunst arrived home, in Waseca, Minnesota, today. He had walked around the whole world! David started his walk on June 20, 1972. Now *that's* a long walk!

1985 Grambling State University beat Prairie View A&M, 27–7, today. The win gave Grambling coach Eddie Robinson his 324th win. That made him the winningest coach in college football history.

October 5, 1992: Philadelphia rookie Eric Lindros scores in his first NHL game.

1992 Philadelphia Flyer rookie Eric Lindros made his NHL debut today. It was a memorable game for him. Eric scored against Pittsburgh Penguin goalie Tom Barrasso 31 seconds into the third period. The goal helped the Flyers to a 3–3 tie. By the end of the season, Eric will have scored 41 goals in 61 games.

6 **1985** New York Yankee pitcher Phil Niekro won the 300th game of his career on the last day of the season. New York beat the Toronto Blue Jays, 8–0. Phil, who was 46 years old, is the oldest pitcher ever to throw a shutout!

1993 The Florida Panthers played their first NHL game today. Panther winger Scott Mellanby scored the first goal in franchise history. The game, against the Chicago Blackhawks, ended in a 4–4 tie.

1993 Michael Jordan jolted basketball fans everywhere today. He made the shocking announcement that he planned to retire from basketball. Michael, who led the Chicago Bulls to three consecutive NBA titles, left the game with the highest scoring average (32.3 points per game) in NBA history. "Air Jordan" had also won seven straight scoring titles and three straight playoff MVP awards.

1916 Georgia Tech University and Cumberland College played the most lopsided game in football history. Georgia Tech scored 63 points — in the first quarter! The final score was Georgia Tech 222, Cumberland 0.

1984 Walter Payton of the Chicago Bears rushed for 154 yards to bring his career total to 12,400 yards. That broke Jim Brown's record for most yards rushing in a career. By the time he retired, Walter would gain 16,726 yards in his 13-year career.

1996 Tiger Woods won his first PGA Tour event. Tiger beat Davis Love III in a sudden-death playoff at the Las Vegas Invitational.

1997 The Atlanta Braves made a record sixth-straight appearance in a League Championship Series. They lost Game 1 to the Florida Marlins and would go on to lose the series in six games.

1904 The 284-mile Vanderbilt Cup auto race was held for the first time. (This became the first U.S. auto race to be held once a year.) George Heath finished first. He raced at an average speed of 52.2 miles per hour!

1956 When Don Larsen of the New York Yankees struck out the last batter of today's World Series game, he had done something no one had ever done before: He had pitched a perfect game in the World Series! Don retired all 27 batters he faced in Game 5.

1957 Baseball fans in Brooklyn, New York, went into mourning today. Their beloved Dodgers announced they were moving to Los Angeles, California. A few months earlier, the New York Giants had announced that they were moving, too.

1988 The Columbia University football team was 0 and 44. It had not won a game in five seasons — until today. Columbia beat Princeton, 16–13, to end college football's longest losing streak.

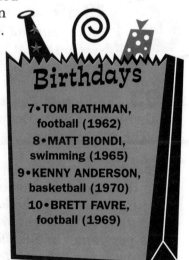

Birthdays

7•TOM RATHMAN,
football (1962)

8•MATT BIONDI,
swimming (1965)

9•KENNY ANDERSON,
basketball (1970)

10•BRETT FAVRE,
football (1969)

9

1904 Poor Jack Chesbro. He was pitching for the New York Highlanders (now the Yankees) on the last day of the season. The score was 1–1 with two outs in the ninth inning. Jack threw a wild pitch and a runner scored. New York lost the game and the pennant.

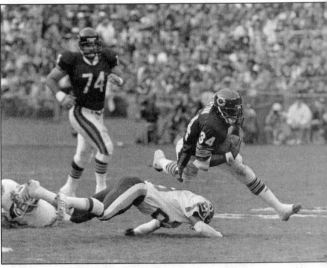

October 7, 1984: Walter Payton sets the NFL record for rushing yards in a career.

1919 The Chicago White Sox lost the World Series today. Eight players were accused of taking bribe money and losing the Series on purpose. All eight men were banned from baseball for life.

1994 Race car driver Mario Andretti sped through his final race today. He finished 19th in the Grand Prix of Monterey, at Laguna Seca Raceway. It was his 407th Indy Car start, an Indy record.

10

1920 There were lots of World Series firsts in today's game. Elmer Smith of the Cleveland Indians hit the first ever Series grand slam. His teammate Jim Bagby hit the first Series homer by a pitcher. And Cleveland second baseman Bill Wambsganss completed an unassisted triple play. The fans sure got their money's worth!

1968 The Detroit Tigers were down three games to one in the 1968 World Series. But the Tigers mounted a stirring comeback to win the Series in seven games over the St. Louis Cardinals. Detroit's Mickey Lolich was the winning pitcher in three games, including today's Game 7.

1987 Columbia University set an embarrassing record today. Its football team lost its 35th game in a row! (The last time Columbia enjoyed a win was on October 15, 1983.)

11 **1890** John Owen won the 100-yard dash at the AAU Track and Field Championships, in Washington, D.C., today. His winning time of 9.8 seconds set a U.S. record and made him the first American to run 100 yards in less than 10 seconds.

1972 What a way to lose! In the fifth game of the National League playoffs, Pittsburgh Pirate pitcher Bob Moose threw a wild pitch. Unfortunately, it was the bottom of the ninth inning and the winning run scored on the play. The Cincinnati Reds won the game and the pennant.

1984 Mario Lemieux took the NHL by storm today. On the ice for his first shift, Mario stripped the puck from All-Star defenseman Ray Bourque of the Boston Bruins. Then, all alone, he skated in on the goalie. Super Mario scored on his first shot on his first shift in his first game!

 **1948** The New York Yankees named Casey Stengel as their manager today. With Casey at the helm, the Yankees will win seven World Series titles from 1949 to 1960!

1967 The dream came to an end today. The Boston Red Sox, who had not won a World Series championship since 1918, had a shot at the crown. But the Sox dropped Game 7 of the World Series to the St. Louis Cardinals.

1991 Quarterback Doug Flutie of the British Columbia Lions passed for 582 yards in today's game, setting a Canadian Football League record for most passing yards in a season. Doug will finish the season with 6,619 yards passing — the best total in pro football history.

Birthdays

11 • STEVE YOUNG, football (1961)
12 • TONY KUBEK, baseball (1936)
13 • JERRY RICE, football (1962)
14 • BETH DANIEL, golf (1956)

13

1960 It was the bottom of the ninth inning in the seventh game of the World Series between the Pittsburgh Pirates and the New York Yankees. The score was tied, 9–9. That's when Pirate Bill Mazeroski hit a home run to give Pittsburgh its first World Series championship since 1925.

1982 On this day, Jim Thorpe was awarded two Olympic gold medals — though he had been dead for 29 years. Jim had won the medals at the 1912 Olympics. But they were taken away after Olympic officials learned that he had once earned money playing a sport. The Olympics were for amateur athletes only (athletes who were not paid), so Jim was disqualified. The Olympic Committee changed its mind today.

October 14, 1990: Jerry Rice ties an NFL record with five touchdown catches!

1993 The Philadelphia Phillies beat the Atlanta Braves, 6–3, to win the National League pennant. (Atlanta was the defending N.L. champ.)

14

1976 It was the fifth and deciding game of the American League Championship Series. With the score tied in the bottom of the ninth inning, Chris Chambliss smacked a home run. The New York Yankees beat the Kansas City Royals to win their first pennant in 12 years.

1990 Jerry Rice tied an NFL record with five touchdown catches in a San Francisco 49er win over the Atlanta Falcons. Jerry caught 13 passes for 225 yards during the game.

1992 Atlanta Brave pinch-hitter Francisco Cabrera drove in two runs with two outs in the ninth inning of today's game against the Pittsburgh Pirates. Those runs gave the Braves the pennant and their second-straight World Series appearance.

15

1925 Today just wasn't Roger Peckinpaugh's day. The Washington Senator shortstop made eight errors in a World Series game against the Pittsburgh Pirates. It's no surprise that the Senators lost the Series.

1988 Kirk Gibson of the Los Angeles Dodgers had won the regular-season MVP award, but a leg injury kept him out of the lineup in Game 1 of the World Series. In the bottom of the ninth inning of today's game, the Dodgers were trailing by one run with two outs. That's when they called on their MVP for help. Kirk hobbled to the plate to pinch-hit. He drilled a 3–2 pitch into the rightfield bleachers for a game-winning home run!

1989 Los Angeles King center Wayne Gretzky scored a goal to break Gordie Howe's NHL career record of 1,850 points. It took Gordie 26 seasons and 1,767 games to set the scoring record. Wayne broke it in his 780th game.

16

1912 Fred Snodgrass made one of the biggest errors in baseball history today. The Giants centerfielder dropped an easy fly ball in the 10th inning of today's World Series game against the Boston Red Sox. Thanks to Fred, the Sox scored two runs and won the Series.

1969 They didn't call them "the Miracle Mets" for nothing. The New York Mets had finished in ninth place the year before. And this year, they were 9 1/2 games out of first as late as August 14. But today, they were playing the Baltimore Orioles for the World Series championship. The New Yorkers stunned Baltimore, winning the Series in five games.

1973 It's never too late to start over. Just ask Victor Morely Lawson. At age 67, he became a jockey. He won his first race today. Victor is the oldest jockey ever to win a race.

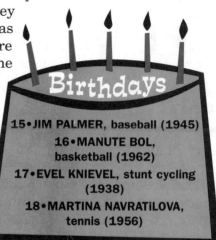

Birthdays

15•JIM PALMER, baseball (1945)

16•MANUTE BOL, basketball (1962)

17•EVEL KNIEVEL, stunt cycling (1938)

18•MARTINA NAVRATILOVA, tennis (1956)

OCTOBER

17 **1989** Game 3 of the 1989 World Series was about to begin. The Oakland A's were playing the Giants at San Francisco's Candlestick Park. Suddenly, the ground began to shake. A powerful earthquake rocked the city, causing the Series to be postponed for 10 days. When play resumed, the A's swept the Giants in four games.

1989 Japan beat the U.S. volleyball team in a three-game series in Japan. It was the first time Japan had beaten the Americans since 1984.

1991 Pittsburgh Penguin Paul Coffey became the highest-scoring defenseman in NHL history. To-day, he broke Denis Potvin's record of 1,053 points.

October 18, 1968: Bob Beamon shatters the world long-jump record.

18 **1924** One of the greatest performances in college football history took place at Memorial Stadium, in Illinois. Michigan had a 20-game winning streak. But Illinois had running back Red Grange on its side. The first six times Red touched the ball, he ran for touchdowns! Illinois won, 39–14.

1968 Bob Beamon leapt into history at the Olympic Games, in Mexico City, Mexico. The American long-jumped a world-record 29 feet, 2½ inches! (Bob's record would stand until August 30, 1991, when Mike Powell jumped 29 feet, 4½ inches.)

1977 Reggie Jackson earned the nickname "Mr. October" on this day. Reggie smacked three home runs in three at-bats in a World Series game. He hit each of his home runs on the first pitch of each at-bat. The Yankees won the Series, beating the Los Angeles Dodgers in six games.

OCTOBER

19

1991 Paula Newby-Fraser of Zimbabwe took the women's title in the Ironman Triathlon for the fourth time in the past six years. Paula finished the 2.4 mile swim, the 112-mile bike race, and the marathon run in 9 hours, 7 minutes, 52 seconds.

1991 Five Sutter brothers — Brent, Darryl, Brian, Rich, and Ron — played in a game between the Chicago Blackhawks and the St. Louis Blues. Up to this point, the Sutters have played in 4,294 NHL games combined. If those games were played back-to-back, it would take more than 50 NHL seasons!

1991 Shawn Graves of Wofford College was born without any chest muscles on the right side of his body. That didn't hold him back. Today, Shawn became the all-time NCAA rushing quarterback: He broke the record of 3,612 career yards!

20

1988 Orel Hershiser led the Los Angeles Dodgers to a five-game World Series triumph over the Oakland A's. Orel pitched the Dodgers to victory in Games 2 and 5 of the Series, allowing just two runs. He was rewarded with a World Series championship and the MVP award.

1993 If it wasn't the strangest World Series game ever played, it was still the highest-scoring. The Toronto Blue Jays beat the Philadelphia Phillies, 15–14, to take a three-games-to-one lead in the Series. It was also the longest game in Series history, lasting 4 hours, 14 minutes.

1994 A Los Angeles Dodger won the National League Rookie of the Year award for the third-straight season. Raul Mondesi won the 1994 honor. He followed teammates Mike Piazza (1993) and Eric Karros (1992). Raul hit .306 with 16 home runs and 56 RBIs.

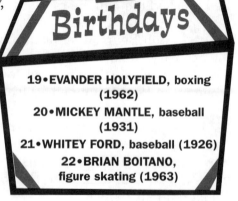

Birthdays

19 • EVANDER HOLYFIELD, boxing (1962)

20 • MICKEY MANTLE, baseball (1931)

21 • WHITEY FORD, baseball (1926)

22 • BRIAN BOITANO, figure skating (1963)

21

1964 Gymnast Larissa Latynina of the Soviet Union won the silver medal in the women's all-around competition at the Olympics, in Tokyo, Japan. In three Olympics, from 1956 to 1964, Larissa won 18 medals. No other athlete has ever won as many.

1973 Los Angeles Ram defensive end Fred Dryer became the first player to record two safeties in one game, a win over the Green Bay Packers. Fred will later star in the TV show *Hunter*.

October 20, 1988: Orel Hershiser leads the Los Angeles Dodgers to the championship.

1989 The University of Houston Cougars beat Southern Methodist, 95–21, in a record-setting college football game. Houston quarterback Andre Ware completed 25 passes for 517 yards and six TDs — all in the first half! In the first quarter, he passed for 340 yards and five TDs, both records.

22

1972 Gene Tenace drove in two runs to give the Oakland A's a 3–2 victory over the Cincinnati Reds in the seventh game of the World Series. Gene, who batted .348, with four homers and nine RBIs, was named the Series MVP. In Game 1, Gene had blasted homers in his first two Series at-bats, a record-setting feat.

1988 Olympic gold medal winners Janet Evans and Matt Biondi received a special honor today. They were named swimmers of the year by United States Swimming, the sport's governing body.

1989 World chess champion Gary Kasparov won a special exhibition. He outsmarted an opponent who had beaten several champs. Who was his opponent? A *computer* named Deep Thought.

 **1968** The world got its first glimpse of George Foreman at the Summer Olympic Games, in Mexico City, Mexico, today. George won the gold medal in the super heavyweight division.

1993 Joe Carter belted a three-run homer in the bottom of the ninth inning today to give the Toronto Blue Jays the World Series championship. It was the second-straight year that the Blue Jays had won the Series.

1994 Dale Earnhardt won the AC Delco 500 at North Carolina Motor Speedway, in Rockingham, North Carolina. With this win, Dale clinched the season's NASCAR points title. It was his seventh Winston Cup title, tying Richard Petty's record. Dale was so happy that he did a lap of honor while standing on the trunk of his car.

 **1857** The first soccer club in the world was founded in England today. The team was called the Sheffield Football Club. (In most of the world, except North America, soccer is called football.)

1908 George Robertson became the first American to win the Vanderbilt Cup auto race on Long Island, New York. George covered the 258-mile course in just over four hours. During the race, his average speed was 64.3 miles per hour.

1993 Eric Metcalf of the Cleveland Browns tied an NFL record when he returned two punts for touchdowns in one game. Cleveland stunned the Pittsburgh Steelers, 28–23.

1994 Greg Maddux of the Atlanta Braves made history by winning a third-straight Cy Young Award. Greg's major league-leading earned run average (ERA) was 1.56 — a full run lower than any other pitcher. His 16–6 record included 10 complete games and three shutouts.

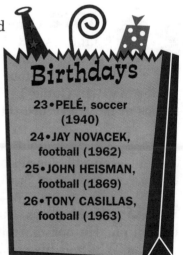

Birthdays

23 • PELÉ, soccer (1940)

24 • JAY NOVACEK, football (1962)

25 • JOHN HEISMAN, football (1869)

26 • TONY CASILLAS, football (1963)

OCTOBER

25 **1964** Minnesota Viking defensive lineman Jim Marshall picked up a fumble and ran 61 yards into the end zone. Unfortunately for Jim, it was his *own* end zone. He scored a 2-point safety for his opponent, the San Francisco 49ers. Minnesota still won, 27–22.

1986 The New York Mets were within one strike of losing the World Series in Game 6. Then, after a series of hits, Boston Red Sox first baseman Bill Buckner let a grounder slip through his legs. The error led to a 6–5 win for the Mets and a Series tie. (The Mets then won Game 7.)

October 26, 1996: The New York Yankees win their first World Series in 18 years.

1990 Evander Holyfield won the world heavyweight boxing title by knocking out James "Buster" Douglas. Buster had shocked the world by defeating Mike Tyson in February. Evander knocked out the champion in three rounds.

26 **1985** New York Knick center Patrick Ewing made his NBA debut and scored 18 points with six rebounds in a loss to the Philadelphia 76ers. Patrick had led Georgetown University to the NCAA finals three times in four years. He was the first overall selection in the June draft.

1996 The New York Yankees capped a great World Series comeback with a 3–2 win in Game 6 against Braves ace Greg Maddux. New York had lost the first two games at home by a combined score of 16–1. The Yanks rallied to win three straight games in Atlanta before returning home for the clincher.

1997 The Florida Marlins defeated the Cleveland Indians, 3–2, to win Game 7 of the World Series! Marlin shortstop Edgar Renteria won the game with an RBI single in the bottom of the 11th inning.

27

1974 The New England Patriots trailed the Minnesota Vikings, 14–10, but the Patriots had the ball on the Minnesota 10. On the last play of the game, Patriot quarterback Jim Plunkett passed to Bob Windsor on the two-yard line. Bob dove into the end zone for a thrilling victory!

1984 Running back Rueben Mayes rushed for 357 yards to lead Washington State University to a win over the University of Oregon, 50–41. Rueben's total set a new college record, beating the old mark of 356, set by Eddie Lee Ivery.

1991 Move over Deion Sanders. You are not the only two-sport star. John Brodie, a former quarterback with the San Francisco 49ers, shot a final-round 68 at the Security Pacific Senior Classic golf tournament, in Los Angeles, California. That score earned John his first pro golf title.

28

1973 Los Angeles Laker center Elmore Smith set an NBA record with 17 blocked shots in a game against the Portland Trail Blazers. Gail Goodrich provided the Lakers with offense, scoring 49 points in the 111–98 win.

1981 After losing the World Series to the New York Yankees in 1977 and 1978, the Los Angeles Dodgers got their revenge. Los Angeles beat New York in the 1981 Series, four games to two.

1984 Grete Waitz of Norway won the New York City Marathon in 2 hours, 29 minutes, 30 seconds. It was Grete's sixth win in seven years. She would go on to win the New York City marathon a record nine times. Grete proved that women could run a marathon. From 1978 through 1990, she won 13 of the 19 marathons she entered and a silver medal at the first women's Olympic marathon, in 1984.

Birthdays

27•PATTY SHEEHAN, golf (1956)

28•BRUCE JENNER, track and field (1949)

29•MIKE GARTNER, hockey (1959)

30•DIEGO MARADONA, soccer (1960)

29

1921 In one of the greatest upsets in college football history, Centre College shocked Harvard, 6–0. It was Harvard's first loss in four years. What was so amazing about Centre? The school had just 300 students!

1950 The Los Angeles Rams scored 41 points in one quarter to crush the Detroit Lions, 65–24. The day wasn't a total loss for Detroit — Lion Wally Triplett set an NFL record for kickoff return yards with 294.

1987 Thomas Hearns knocked out Juan Roldan in the fourth round of their middleweight boxing match. With that victory, Thomas became the first boxer ever to win titles in four different weight categories. "The Hit Man" had held titles in the welterweight, super welterweight, and light heavyweight divisions.

October 28, 1984: Grete Waitz wins the New York City Marathon for the sixth time!

30

1954 BZZZZZZZ! That's the sound of the 24-second shot clock going off for the first time. Until 1954, pro basketball teams could hold on to the ball as long as they wanted before shooting. That made for some very low-scoring games.

1974 Muhammad Ali used a weird strategy, which he called the "rope-a-dope," to win the heavyweight boxing title from George Foreman. He leaned against the ropes and let George punch him until George's arms were tired. Then he knocked George out.

1993 The first official bout between women boxers took place today in Lynnwood, Washington. Dallas Malloy, a 16-year-old, outboxed 21-year-old Heather Poyner. Dallas won the bout in three 2-minute rounds.

31 **1986** Julius "Doctor J" Erving announced that he would retire at the end of the season. Julius, who had played for the New York Nets of the old ABA, was now playing for the Philadelphia 76ers of the NBA. In 16 seasons, he had led the Nets to two ABA titles and the 76ers to one NBA title.

1987 Chris Antley became the first jockey to win nine races in a single day. But there was a catch. He rode the winning horses at two different race tracks, in two different states! He was in the saddle aboard four winners at Aqueduct, in New York, then crossed the Hudson River to New Jersey to ride five winners at the Meadowlands.

1993 Mark Allen won his record fifth-consecutive Ironman Triathlon, in Kailua-Kona, Hawaii. He finished the 2.4-mile swim, the 112-mile bike ride, and the 26.2-mile run in 8 hours, 7 minutes, 46 seconds. That was a record time!

Birthdays

31•BILL FRALIC,
football (1962)
31•FRED McGRIFF,
baseball (1963)
31•BLUE EDWARDS,
basketball (1965)

NOVEMBER

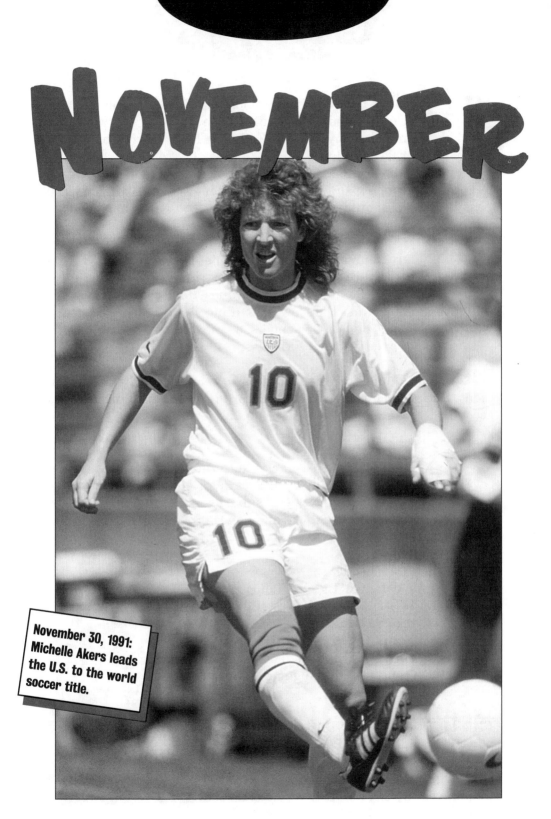

November 30, 1991: Michelle Akers leads the U.S. to the world soccer title.

1 **1913** Thanks to several long passes to star player (and future coaching legend) Knute Rockne, Notre Dame bombed Army, 35–13. Fighting Irish quarterback Gus Dorais completed 14 of 17 passes for 243 yards. The forward pass had become legal in 1906, but many teams ignored this new play. It was not until Notre Dame's big win that the forward pass became a popular offensive strategy. And with that, modern football was born.

1959 Picture yourself as a hockey goalie. Now imagine that you aren't wearing a face mask. Pretty scary, huh? That's how goaltenders defended their nets until Jacques Plante came along. In tonight's game against the New York Rangers, the Montreal goalie wore a mask that he had designed. The mask didn't get in his way — Jacques stopped 28 of 29 Ranger shots.

1992 Lisa Ondieki of Australia won the New York City Marathon today. She set the women's course record in 2 hours, 24 minutes, 40 seconds.

2  **1895** The first official auto race in the U.S. was held in Chicago, Illinois. Six cars raced along the 54-mile course through city and suburban streets. A heavy snowstorm blew into town, and none of the cars was able to finish the race!

1969 In an air battle, the New Orleans Saints defeated the St. Louis Cardinals, 51–42. Quarterbacks Bill Kilmer of the Saints and Charlie Johnson of the Cardinals each tossed six touchdown passes. The 12 touchdown passes in one game set an NFL record.

1990 In the first NBA game played outside North America, the Phoenix Suns defeated the Utah Jazz, 119–96. The game was played in Tokyo, Japan.

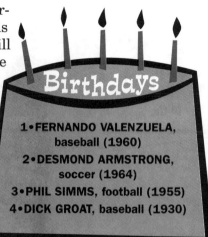

Birthdays

1•FERNANDO VALENZUELA, baseball (1960)

2•DESMOND ARMSTRONG, soccer (1964)

3•PHIL SIMMS, football (1955)

4•DICK GROAT, baseball (1930)

3

1961 The Boston Patriots football team beat the Dallas Texans on the last play of today's game. The Dallas quarterback had thrown the ball to a receiver. A defender batted it away, ending the game. The defender was a fan who had sneaked onto the field! He ran away before the refs saw him.

1973 Jay Miller of Brigham Young University set a college football record by catching 22 passes for 263 yards in today's game. No player had ever pulled in that many passes in one game, and no one has done it since.

1990 The University of Houston defeated Texas Christian University, 56–35, in one of football's greatest passing shows. Houston quarterback David Klingler completed 36 passes for seven touchdowns and TCU quarterback Matt Vogler completed 44 passes for five TDs!

November 1, 1959: Goalie Jacques Plante will start wearing a mask.

4

1971 Just two weeks into the NBA season, Los Angeles Laker superstar Elgin Baylor announced his retirement. A 6' 5" forward, Elgin was an 11-time All-Star who averaged 27.4 points per game.

1989 A horse named Sunday Silence stuck his neck out and narrowly beat Easy Goer in the Breeders' Cup Classic today.

1990 The Washington Redskins were in trouble. Their top two quarterbacks were hurt, and the Skins trailed the Detroit Lions, 38–24, in the fourth quarter. That's when Jeff Rutledge, the third-string quarterback, went to work. He threw a touchdown pass and ran for another TD, tying the game with 18 seconds left. (Jeff also led the drive that set up the game-winning field goal in overtime.)

5

1911 Calbraith P. Rodgers became the first man to fly a plane across the United States. He did it in a plane that had been designed by the Wright brothers. After a few crash landings, Calbraith was safely across the country. It took him 49 days to make the flight from New York City to Pasadena, California. Nowadays, it would take about six hours.

1993 Jamal Mashburn placed his size 16 sneakers on the hardwood court and became the youngest player in Dallas Maverick history. As a junior, 20-year-old Jamal had led Kentucky to the Final Four. He was the Mavericks' first-round selection in the NBA draft.

1994 At age 45, George Foreman shocked the sports world and regained the heavyweight boxing crown he had lost two decades earlier. He floored defending champ Michael Moorer in the 10th round. George is the oldest champ in boxing history.

6

1972 The first official Ultimate Frisbee game was played in New Brunswick, New Jersey, today. Rutgers University beat Princeton University, 29–27. (Played with a flying disk, Ultimate Frisbee is a team sport that is a lot like football.)

1974 Los Angeles Dodger reliever Mike Marshall became the first relief pitcher to win the Cy Young Award. Mike had 15 wins and 21 saves for the season. He appeared in a major league record 106 games and pitched a record 209 innings of relief.

1993 Evander Holyfield regained the heavyweight boxing title with a 12-round decision over defending champion Riddick Bowe. The fight was delayed for 21 minutes in the seventh round by a parachutist who tried to drop into the ring and got tangled up.

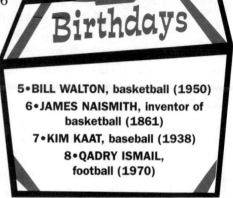

Birthdays

5•BILL WALTON, basketball (1950)
6•JAMES NAISMITH, inventor of basketball (1861)
7•KIM KAAT, baseball (1938)
8•QADRY ISMAIL, football (1970)

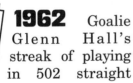
7

1962 Goalie Glenn Hall's streak of playing in 502 straight complete games ended when he had to leave a game with a bad back. He hadn't missed a start for seven seasons!

1975 The Boston Bruins traded Phil Esposito, a two-time NHL Most Valuable Player, to the New York Rangers. Espo was the first player to score 70 goals and 100 points in a season. A center, he scored 717 goals in a career that lasted from 1963 to 1981.

November 7, 1991: Magic Johnson announces he is retiring from the NBA.

1991 Magic Johnson announced his retirement from the NBA because he had tested positive for HIV, the virus that causes AIDS. In a dozen years with the Los Angeles Lakers, Magic led the team to five NBA championships. He was an eight-time All-Star and the league's Most Valuable Player three times.

8

1966 Frank Robinson of the Baltimore Orioles was named the American League's Most Valuable Player. Frank won the Triple Crown (topping the league in batting average, home runs, and RBIs) and led his team to a sweep of the Los Angeles Dodgers in the World Series. Frank, who had won the MVP with the Cincinnati Reds, in 1961, is the only player to have won the award in both leagues.

1970 New Orleans Saints kicker Tom Dempsey, who was born with half a right foot, booted a 63-yard field goal, the longest in NFL history. It gave the Saints a 19–17 win over the Detroit Lions.

1987 St. Louis trailed Tampa Bay, 28–3, after three quarters. But the Cardinals shocked the Bucs by scoring 28 unanswered points in the fourth quarter. St. Louis won, 31–28!

1912 Dwight D. Eisenhower's college football career came to an end today. Playing for the U.S. Military Academy, Dwight broke his kneecap in a game against Tufts University. He decided to give up the sport. Dwight will go on to get good jobs after graduation: He will be the commander of the American troops in Europe during World War II, and become President of the United States.

1991 San Diego State running back Marshall Faulk rushed for 174 yards and a touchdown in the Aztecs' 42–32 win over Colorado State. Marshall tied Emmitt Smith's NCAA record for freshmen by reaching the 1,000-yard rushing mark in only seven games.

1993 Barry Bonds won the National League's Most Valuable Player award for the third time in four years. The San Francisco Giants leftfielder batted .336, with 123 RBIs and 46 home runs for the season.

10

1985 Mark Duper caught a 50-yard touchdown pass from quarterback Dan Marino with 41 seconds left in the game to give the Miami Dolphins a 21–17 win over the New York Jets. Mark caught eight passes in the game for a total of 217 yards. Super, Duper!

1990 No NBA team has ever scored 200 points in a game, but the Phoenix Suns came close today. They got off to an amazing start, scoring 107 points in the first half. They slowed down in the second, finishing with 173. It was more than enough to beat the Denver Nuggets, who scored 143 points of their own.

1991 Washington Redskin quarterback Mark Rypien hurled six touchdown passes to tie a team record. He also ran for another score in a 56–17 win over the Atlanta Falcons. Mark would lead the Redskins to the Super Bowl title and be named NFL MVP.

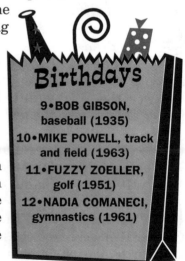

Birthdays

9•BOB GIBSON, baseball (1935)

10•MIKE POWELL, track and field (1963)

11•FUZZY ZOELLER, golf (1951)

12•NADIA COMANECI, gymnastics (1961)

NOVEMBER

11

1944 Led by the backfield heroics of Doc Blanchard and Glenn Davis, the U.S. Military Academy football team blasted the University of Notre Dame, 59–0. The loss was the worst in Fighting Irish history.

1988 The University of Dallas beat John Brown University, 76–68, to end college basketball's longest losing streak. Dallas hadn't won in 86 games!

1990 Kansas City Chief Derrick Thomas set an NFL record with seven quarterback sacks in a game against the Seattle Seahawks. On the game's final play, Derrick had Seahawk quarterback Dave Krieg in his grasp for sack number eight. But Dave wriggled free and threw the winning touchdown pass.

November 10, 1991: NFL MVP Mark Rypien passes for six touchdowns.

12

1892 William "Pudge" Heffelfinger became the first professional football player today. He was paid $500 to play one game with the Allegheny Athletic Association against its fierce rival, the Pittsburgh Athletic Club.

1920 Baseball owners hired the sport's first commissioner, a former judge named Kenesaw Mountain Landis. Judge Landis ruled baseball for 23 years. His most famous act was to ban eight Chicago White Sox players from baseball. The players were accused of taking money from gamblers to lose the 1919 World Series on purpose.

1964 Paula Murphy of California set a women's land-speed record today. On Utah's Bonneville Salt Flats, she drove her jet-powered car 226.37 miles per hour!

13 **1964** St. Louis Hawk forward Bob Pettit became the first player in NBA history to score 20,000 points in a career. After 11 years in the league, Bob retired with 20,880 points. He averaged 26.4 points and 16.2 rebounds per game and was named league MVP twice.

1985 Lynette Woodard, an All-America basketball player at the University of Kansas, became the first woman to play for the Harlem Globetrotters. Lynette, who won a gold medal as a member of the 1984 U.S. Olympic Women's Basketball Team, scored seven points in her first game with the Globetrotters.

1987 The Washington Bullets made 60 free throws in 69 attempts in today's game against the New York Knicks. That broke a 38-year-old NBA record for most free throws attempted by a team in one game. The Bullets defeated the Knicks, 108–101.

14 **1889** The first golf course in the United States was opened in Yonkers, New York. The six-hole course was built on a cow pasture. Fortunately, all the cows had been removed long before the first golfer teed off.

1943 In a victory over the Detroit Lions, Washington Redskin Sammy Baugh set a record that will probably never be broken. Sammy, who was the Redskins' quarterback, defensive end, and punter, became the only player in NFL history to pass for four touchdowns and intercept four passes in one game. (Back then, players often played both offense and defense.)

1993 The Miami Dolphins defeated the Philadelphia Eagles, 19–14, giving Dolphin coach Don Shula his 325th coaching win. Coach Shula passed George Halas on the all-time list to become the winningest coach in NFL history.

Birthdays

13•MEL STOTTLEMYRE, baseball (1941)

14•LIONEL SIMMONS, basketball (1968)

15•GREG ANTHONY, basketball (1967)

16•OKSANA BAIUL, figure skating (1977)

15

1964 Mickey Wright set a new women's record by firing a 62 in the first round of the Tall City Open, in Midland, Texas. Mickey will win 82 titles in her career to rank second for all time.

1992 NASCAR legend Richard Petty, 55, raced for the final time in his 35-year career. A fiery crash ended his chances of going out a winner, but Richard is still the all-time winningest stock-car driver.

1994 Martina Navratilova, the greatest woman tennis player in history, played her final singles match today. Martina retired from singles competition after a match against Gabriela Sabatini, during the Virginia Slims Championship in New York City.

November 13, 1985: Lynette Woodard becomes the first female Harlem Globetrotter.

16

1957 The University of Notre Dame upset the University of Oklahoma, 7–0, snapping college football's longest winning streak. The Sooners had won a record 47 consecutive games, including two national titles.

1960 Los Angeles Laker forward Elgin Baylor broke his own record for most points in a basketball game. The forward scored an amazing 71 points against the New York Knicks. (Elgin's record will be shattered when Wilt Chamberlain racks up 100 points in a single game.)

1993 Today, Jay Bell of the Pittsburgh Pirates won the National League Gold Glove award for fielding excellence at shortstop. He broke St. Louis Cardinal Ozzie Smith's 14-year lock on the award.

1956 Jim Brown was an All-America lacrosse player at Syracuse University. But he was even better at football. In a game against Colgate University on this day, Jim scored an NCAA record 43 points on six touchdowns and 7 extra points. Jim later played nine seasons in the NFL with the Cleveland Browns. He retired as the league's all-time leading rusher.

1968 The New York Jets were leading the Oakland Raiders late in today's game. TV viewers were glued to their sets as time ticked away. But they didn't see the end of the game. Instead, the TV network switched to the movie *Heidi*. In the game's thrilling finish, Oakland scored twice in nine seconds and beat the Jets, 43–32! Since then, even when football games run long, TV stations show the ending.

1990 In a game against Eastern Washington University, quarterback David Klingler of the University of Houston threw 11 touchdown passes to set a college football single-game record. By season's end, David would break or tie an amazing 33 NCAA records!

1940 Cornell University beat Dartmouth University in a football game today. But, after realizing that the referee had made a mistake, the Cornell players decided they did not deserve the victory and gave the win to Dartmouth.

1966 Sandy Koufax retired today because of an arm injury. The 30-year-old pitcher had won 27 games for the Los Angeles Dodgers during the season. Between 1962 and 1966, Sandy was the most dominating pitcher in baseball. During those five seasons, the lefthander won five ERA titles, four strikeout titles, three Cy Young Awards, one MVP, and pitched four no-hitters.

1990 At the Virginia Slims Championship, Monica Seles and Gabriela Sabatini played the first five-set women's tennis match in 89 years. Monica won.

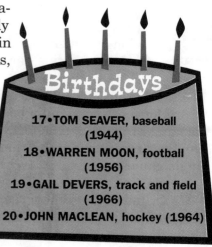

Birthdays

17•TOM SEAVER, baseball (1944)

18•WARREN MOON, football (1956)

19•GAIL DEVERS, track and field (1966)

20•JOHN MACLEAN, hockey (1964)

19

1978 The New York Giants were leading the Philadelphia Eagles, 12–10, with 20 seconds left in the game. Giants quarterback Joe Pisarcik only needed to take the snap, drop his knee to the ground, and the Giants would win. But Joe fumbled trying to make a handoff! Eagle defender Herman Edwards picked up the ball and ran for the winning score.

1989 The U.S. soccer team nipped the team from Trinidad and Tobago, 1–0. It was a very big win. The U.S. team now qualified for its first World Cup appearance in almost 40 years.

1989 Steffi Graf ended an amazing year by defeating Martina Navratilova in the Virginia Slims Championship. The victory gave Steffi her 14th title and an 86–2 match record for the season — the second best ever!

November 18, 1990: Monica Seles plays a five-set match.

20

1977 Chicago Bear running back Walter Payton rushed for a record 275 yards today to lead the Bears to a 10–7 victory over the Minnesota Vikings. Walter got the record with a 58-yard run in the final minutes.

1982 The University of California football team was trailing Stanford University by 1 point and time was running out. The Stanford band started marching onto the field. But California was not finished yet. The Golden Bears put together an amazing kick return play, and California's Kevin Moen knocked over a Stanford trombone player to score the winning touchdown.

1991 Auto-racer Michael Andretti was named Driver of the Year. His little brother, Jeff, won Rookie of the Year honors. (Their father, Mario, won the first Driver of the Year award, in 1967.)

21

1971 What a period! The New York Rangers set an NHL record by scoring eight goals in the third period of a game against the California Golden Seals. New York won, 12–1.

1987 Lorraine Constanzo of the U.S. achieved the greatest powerlift by a woman, with a squat of 628 pounds! (In a squat, the lifter stands with the barbell at shoulder height, drops into a squat position, pauses, and stands again.) Lorraine lifted more than three times her body weight.

1993 The University of North Carolina women's soccer team won its eighth-straight NCAA title with a 6–0 win over George Mason University. The Lady Tar Heels have won 11 championships in the past 12 years.

22

1950 The lowest-scoring game in professional basketball history was played today. The Fort Wayne Pistons nipped the Minneapolis Lakers, 19–18. (The 24-second shot clock wouldn't exist for four more years, so teams could hold the ball as long as they wanted. The Pistons "froze" the ball to keep it away from Laker star George Mikan.)

1981 Quarterback Warren Moon led the Edmonton Eskimos to their fourth-straight Canadian Football League title. Edmonton downed Ottawa, 26–23, in the Grey Cup championship game. Warren played six seasons in Canada. His team won the Grey Cup five straight times.

1986 Mike Tyson scored a second-round knockout over Trevor Berbick to win the World Boxing Council heavyweight title. At the age of 20 years, 5 months, Mike became the youngest champion in the history of heavyweight boxing.

Birthdays

21 • KEN GRIFFEY, JUNIOR, baseball (1969)

22 • BILLIE JEAN KING, tennis (1943)

23 • VIN BAKER, basketball (1971)

24 • OSCAR ROBERTSON, basketball (1938)

NOVEMBER

23 **1984** Boston College quarterback Doug Flutie helped make today's game against the University of Miami one of the most exciting in college football history. Miami was leading Boston College, 45–41, with seconds left to play. On fourth down, Doug threw a 64-yard pass into the end zone. The ball came down into the arms of receiver Gerard Phelan. B.C. won, 47–45!

1991 University of Kansas tailback Tony Sands broke the NCAA single-game rushing mark with 396 yards today. Tony, who scored four touchdowns in the game, carried the ball 58 times — another record. Kansas crushed Missouri, 53–29.

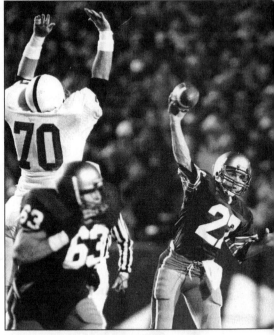

November 23, 1984: Doug Flutie passed into the history books.

1992 Temple University made Ron Dickerson the first African-American head coach of a major college football team.

24 **1949** The Syracuse Nationals and the Anderson (Indiana) Packers played the longest NBA game ever. Syracuse won after five overtime periods. Two years later, another game went into *six* overtime periods.

1960 Philadelphia's Wilt Chamberlain nabbed an NBA-record 55 rebounds in a game against the Boston Celtics. Wilt was the game's greatest rebounder — and a tremendous scorer. He is the all-time leader in career rebounds (23,924) and rebounding average (22.9).

1962 Swimmer Dawn Fraser was the first woman to break the one-minute barrier in the 100-meter freestyle. Today, the Australian swimmer lowered her world record to 59.5 seconds. Dawn is the only swimmer ever to win the gold medal in the same event at three straight Olympic Games.

NOVEMBER

25 **1980** Five months after defeating Sugar Ray Leonard in their first bout, welterweight champ Roberto Duran quit in the middle of the rematch. Roberto turned his back on Sugar Ray in the 8th round and stopped fighting.

1981 Milwaukee Brewer Rollie Fingers became the first relief pitcher ever to win a league MVP award. Rollie, who saved a league-leading 28 games, also won the Cy Young Award. Since then, two other relievers have won the rare double: Detroit's Willie Hernandez, in 1984, and Oakland's Dennis Eckersley, in 1992.

1993 The Miami Dolphins beat the Dallas Cowboys, 16–14, in a strange game. It looked as if the Cowboys had won after they blocked a field goal try in the final seconds. Cowboy Leon Lett tried to recover the ball but fumbled. Miami fell on the ball at the one-yard line with three seconds left. The Dolphins kicked the winning field goal on the next play.

26 **1963** Quarterback Roger Staubach of the U.S. Naval Academy won the Heisman Trophy as college football's best player. Because of his Navy commitment, Roger would serve his country for four years before joining the NFL. He played for the Dallas Cowboys from 1969 to 1979, leading them to Super Bowl titles in 1971 and 1977.

1975 Boston Red Sox outfielder Fred Lynn had an amazing rookie season, winning Rookie of the Year and American League Most Valuable Player honors. Fred is the only player to win the MVP in his first major league season. He led the Sox to the World Series with a .331 average, 21 homers, and 105 RBIs.

1989 Willie "Flipper" Anderson of the Los Angeles Rams set an NFL record with 336 receiving yards on 15 catches in a game against the New Orleans Saints. Down 17–3 with three minutes to play, the Rams scored 17 points to win, 20–17.

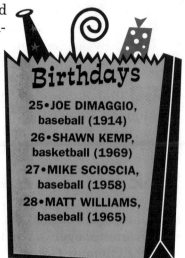

Birthdays

25 • JOE DIMAGGIO, baseball (1914)

26 • SHAWN KEMP, basketball (1969)

27 • MIKE SCIOSCIA, baseball (1958)

28 • MATT WILLIAMS, baseball (1965)

27

1960 Detroit Red Wing Gordie Howe made an assist in today's game. The point brought his career total to 1,000!

1980 The Chicago Bears and Detroit Lions were tied after regulation. When Chicago won the coin flip to begin overtime, they chose to receive the kick-off. Dave Williams returned the kick for a touchdown and an instant victory.

November 27, 1960: Gordie Howe scores the 1,000th point of his great career.

1990 Skier Tamara McKinney announced her retirement because of a bad knee injury. The 28-year-old was the best American woman ski racer ever. In 13 years on the U.S. ski team, Tamara won 18 World Cup races and a gold medal in the combined event at the 1989 World Championships, in Vail, Colorado.

28

1925 Montreal Canadien goaltender Georges Vezina collapsed in net during an NHL game today. He was found to have tuberculosis, a disease of the lungs that took his life four months later. Each year, the NHL's top goalie receives the Vezina Trophy. It is named in honor of Georges.

1929 Ernie Nevers scored all 40 points for the Chicago Cardinals in a 40–6 victory over the Chicago Bears. His 40 points scored in one game remains the longest-standing record in NFL history.

1981 Alabama fought back from a fourth quarter hole to defeat Auburn, 28–17. It was coach Paul "Bear" Bryant's 315th career coaching victory. The Bear was now football's all-time winningest coach. One year later, Coach Bryant would retire with 323 wins. His Alabama teams won six national titles, 15 bowl games, and had four undefeated seasons.

NOVEMBER

1987 Fourteen-year-old Chrissy Wolking set a women's bowling record by rolling 173 games in 18 hours without a break. The Riva, Maryland, resident bowled about 10 games an hour!

1989 The University of Oklahoma basketball team scored 97 points tonight — in the first half! The Sooners set an NCAA record for most points in a half. They flattened the team from U.S. International University, 173–101.

1992 Pittsburgh Steeler Barry Foster rushed for 102 yards in a 21–9 win over Cincinnati. He set a club record for yards rushing in a season. By year's end, Barry will have rushed for 1,690 yards — tops in the AFC.

1979 Boxer Sugar Ray Leonard won the welterweight championship on a technical knockout over Wilfred Benitez. Sugar Ray knocked Wilfred down in the 15th round, and the referee stopped the bout. This championship was Sugar Ray's first. He would go on to win four others in four different weight divisions.

1987 Los Angeles Raider running back Bo Jackson set a team record with 221 yards rushing on just 18 carries. Bo caught one touchdown pass and ran for two others, including a run of 91 yards. L.A. whipped the Seattle Seahawks, 37–14.

1991 The U.S. women's soccer team won the first women's world championship today. The Americans beat Norway in the final, 2–1. During the tournament, forward Michelle Akers scored 10 goals, and forward Carin Gabarra was named most outstanding player. The U.S. women are the only U.S. soccer team ever to win an international tournament.

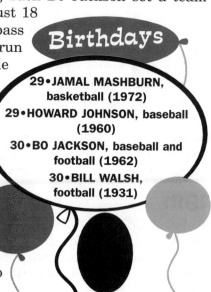

Birthdays

29•JAMAL MASHBURN, basketball (1972)

29•HOWARD JOHNSON, baseball (1960)

30•BO JACKSON, baseball and football (1962)

30•BILL WALSH, football (1931)

DECEMBER

December 19, 1989: Muggsy Bogues passes for 18 assists in an NBA game.

1

1961 Wilt Chamberlain of the Philadelphia Warriors scored 60 points in a game against the Los Angeles Lakers. It wasn't the first time Wilt lit up the scoreboard, and it wouldn't be the last. In his career, Wilt will score 60 or more points in a game 32 times, an NBA record.

1990 It was a good news, bad news day for Ty Detmer. The Brigham Young University quarterback, who passed for an NCAA single-season record 5,188 yards, was named the Heisman Trophy winner. Hours later, Ty threw four interceptions in an embarrassing 59–28 loss to the University of Hawaii.

1990 The U.S. tennis doubles team of Rick Leach and Jim Pugh defeated an Australian duo to bring the Davis Cup to the U.S. for the first time since 1982. Davis Cup is an international tennis competition. Since the Davis Cup began in 1900, the U.S. has won the Cup a record 30 times.

2

1975 Ohio State University running back Archie Griffin won the Heisman Trophy for the second-straight year. He is the only player ever to win the award twice. Archie, who set an NCAA record with 31 straight 100-yard rushing games, finished college with 5,176 yards rushing.

1990 Stanford University freshman Summer Sanders was on a hot streak at the U.S. Open swimming championships, in Indianapolis, Indiana, today. Summer won the 200-meter butterfly in 2 minutes, 12.33 seconds. It was her third individual title.

1993 The Houston Rockets beat the New York Knicks to bring their season record to 15–0. That tied a 45-year-old NBA record for the most wins to start a season. (The next night, the Rockets dropped a game to Atlanta.) The Rockets went on to win the 1993–94 NBA title.

Birthdays

1•LEE TREVINO, golf (1939)
2•MONICA SELES, tennis (1973)
3•KATARINA WITT, figure skating (1965)
4•SERGEI BUBKA, track and field (1963)

3

1950 Tom Fears of the Los Angeles Rams set an NFL record by catching 18 passes in one game.

1966 Lew Alcindor played in his first varsity game with the University of California at Los Angeles (UCLA). He scored a school-record 56 points! UCLA beat the University of Southern California, 105–90. (Lew will later change his name to Kareem Abdul-Jabbar.)

1987 The Boston Bruins honored hockey great Phil Esposito by retiring his number, 7. The only problem was, the team's current captain, Ray Bourque, wore number 7, too. During the ceremony, Ray took off his jersey. Under it he wore a jersey with a new number, 77.

December 4, 1988: Oklahoma State's Barry Sanders rushes for 332 yards.

4

1936 Norman Skelly and John Shefuga finished a cross-country trip today. They roller-skated all the way from Boston, Massachusetts, to Los Angeles, California! It took them about two months.

1960 Baltimore Colt quarterback Johnny Unitas extended his NFL-record-setting streak by throwing two touchdown passes in today's game. That gave Johnny at least one TD pass in 47 straight games! The streak will end the following week when the Colts lose.

1988 Oklahoma State University running back Barry Sanders rushed for 332 yards to lead his team to a 45–42 win over Texas Tech. Barry finished the season with the NCAA records for most yards rushing (2,628) and most touchdowns (37) in a season. The previous day, Barry was named winner of the Heisman Trophy!

5

1868 A new kind of school opened in New York City today — a bicycle school! It was the first in the country. Students learned to ride, race, and take care of their bikes. (In the 1860's, bicycles were built with a large front wheel and a small back wheel and were tough to handle.)

1976 The University of San Francisco captured the NCAA soccer title for the second year in a row. They defeated Indiana University, 1–0. It was the Hoosiers' first loss of the season. Until the championship game, they had won 20 games in a row.

1978 After 16 seasons with the Cincinnati Reds, free-agent Pete Rose signed a contract with the Philadelphia Phillies. Pete would help the Phillies win the World Series in 1980. He returned to the Reds as a player-manager in 1984.

6

1984 Helena Sukova snapped tennis great Martina Navratilova's record winning streak today. It happened in the semi-finals of the Australian Open. Martina had won 74 singles matches in a row, including the French Open, Wimbledon, and the U.S. Open. Today's loss ended her hopes of winning the Grand Slam. It was just her third defeat in 167 matches.

1987 In leading his team to victory over the Green Bay Packers, San Francisco 49er quarterback Joe Montana completed 22 passes in a row! That broke Kenny Anderson's record of 20 consecutive passes, set with the Cincinnati Bengals in 1983.

1992 Jerry Rice of the San Francisco 49ers caught a touchdown pass from Steve Young in the fourth quarter of today's game. The touchdown helped the 49ers beat the Miami Dolphins, 27–3. It was the 101st TD catch of Jerry's career, the most in NFL history!

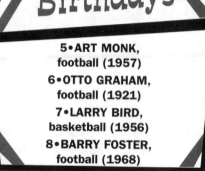

Birthdays

5•ART MONK,
football (1957)

6•OTTO GRAHAM,
football (1921)

7•LARRY BIRD,
basketball (1956)

8•BARRY FOSTER,
football (1968)

7

1963 The instant replay was born today. The CBS television network used it during a game between the U.S. Military Academy (Army) and the U.S. Naval Academy. With about seven minutes left to play, Army quarterback Rollie Stichweh faked a handoff and ran for a touchdown. That touchdown was shown again to viewers at home as TV's first instant replay.

1990 The NHL got a little bigger today. Two expansion teams joined the league: the Ottawa Senators (in Ottawa, Canada) and the Tampa Bay Lightning (in Tampa, Florida).

1991 AJ Kitt of the U.S. won the men's downhill skiing event at the World Cup competition in Val d'Isere, France. He was the first American to win a World Cup ski event in seven years.

December 7, 1991: Downhill skier AJ Kitt outraces the world.

8

1940 The most lopsided game in NFL history was played today. In the NFL Championship Game, the Chicago Bears demolished the Washington Redskins, 73–0! The visiting Bears scored eight touchdowns on offense and three on defense.

1987 Hockey goalies are expected to stop goals, not score them. But in a game against the Boston Bruins, goalie Ron Hextall of the Philadelphia Flyers took a shot at an empty net. He scored! Ron became the first NHL goalie ever to score a goal. (He also scored a goal in a playoff game two years later.)

1992 In a game against the Chicago Bulls, Dominique Wilkins of the Atlanta Hawks hit 23 free throws without a miss — an NBA single-game record!

DECEMBER

9

1934 Things looked bad for the New York Giants in today's NFL Championship Game. They trailed the Chicago Bears, 10–3, at the half. To make things worse, the players kept slipping because their cleats couldn't dig into the frozen ground. When New York took the field in the third quarter, they wore sneakers to keep from slipping. The Giants went on to win, 30–13.

1949 The NFL expanded to 13 teams today. The league's newest franchises were the Cleveland Browns, Baltimore Colts, and San Francisco 49ers. These teams had been playing in the All-America Football Conference (AAFC). That league lasted just four years.

1978 The Women's Professional Basketball League was the first pro basketball league for women. Today, the WPBL played its first game. The Chicago Hustle beat the Milwaukee Does, 92–87. (The league lasted until 1981.)

1938 American-style football came to Europe today. Two U.S. all-star football teams played an exhibition game in Paris, France. Only 2,000 people showed up to watch the game.

1990 The University of North Carolina and the University of Kentucky, two of the most celebrated college-basketball teams in history, squared off in a historic meeting. The Tar Heels and the Wildcats were tied for the all-time lead in college basketball victories, at 1,483. In a battle to break the tie, Carolina came out on top, 84–81.

1993 Rodeo cowboy Ty Murray won his fifth straight all-around championship at the National Finals Rodeo, in Las Vegas, Nevada. In 1989, at age 20, Ty had become the youngest all-around world champion in rodeo history. (He will win the world title every year through 1994.)

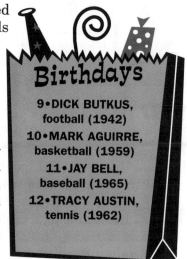

Birthdays

9•DICK BUTKUS, football (1942)

10•MARK AGUIRRE, basketball (1959)

11•JAY BELL, baseball (1965)

12•TRACY AUSTIN, tennis (1962)

11

1977 The Tampa Bay Buccaneers finally won a game, beating the New Orleans Saints, 33–14. The Bucs joined the NFL as an expansion team two years earlier. Since then, they lost 26 games in a row!

1993 University of Louisville center Clifford Rozier hit all 15 of his shots in a victory over Eastern Kentucky University. The junior set an NCAA record for shooting accuracy.

1993 Quarterback Charlie Ward of Florida State won the Heisman Trophy today. He will be the first Heisman winner in 35 years not to be selected in the NFL draft. But the New York Knicks will pick Charlie in the first round of the *NBA* draft!

December 12, 1981: Muhammad Ali fights for the last time in his boxing career.

12

1965 Chicago Bear running back Gale Sayers burst into the NFL record book by scoring six touchdowns in a game. Gale had 113 yards rushing, 89 yards receiving, and 134 yards returning kicks. His combined total of 336 yards still ranks as the fifth highest of all time. He lifted the Bears to a 61–20 blowout over the San Francisco 49ers.

1981 Muhammad Ali fought the final fight of his 20-year boxing career — and lost, to Trevor Berbick in a decision. Muhammad was the only boxer to win the heavyweight title three different times.

1993 Jerome Bettis, the rookie fullback for the Los Angeles Rams, rushed for 212 yards, as the Rams beat the New Orleans Saints, 23–20. Jerome became the eighth rookie in NFL history to rush for more than 200 yards in a game.

DECEMBER

13

1978 Dave Cowens of the Boston Celtics was thrown out of the same game twice! First, Dave, who was the Celtics' player-coach, was whistled by the referee for his sixth foul. He was automatically out of the game as a player. Later on, the referee ejected Coach Cowens for arguing a call.

1983 Both defenses were demolished when the Detroit Pistons faced the Denver Nuggets today. Detroit won the game, 186–184, in triple overtime! Four players scored 40 or more points. The 360 combined points by both teams set an NBA record. (The 136 field goals and 93 assists were also records.)

1995 Paul Coffey of the Detroit Red Wings set up teammate Igor Larionov's goal in the first period of a 3–1 win against the Chicago Blackhawks. With that pass, Paul became the first defenseman in NHL history to tally 1,000 career assists.

14

1982 Los Angeles King sharp-shooter Marcel Dionne became the ninth player in NHL history to score 500 career goals. Marcel played with Detroit, Los Angeles, and New York, from 1971 to 1989. He finished his career with 731 goals and 1,771 points, to rank third in each for all time.

1984 Los Angeles Ram halfback Eric Dickerson gained 98 yards against the San Francisco 49ers in the season's final game. That increased his rushing total to 2,105 yards, the most ever in a single season. The week before, Eric had broken the record of 2,003, set by O.J. Simpson in 1973.

1988 Finally, the Heat was on. After losing its first 17 games, the Miami Heat got its first win in franchise history, squeaking past the Los Angeles Clippers, 89–88.

Birthdays

13•SERGEI FEDOROV, hockey (1969)

14•ANTHONY MASON, basketball (1966)

15•MO VAUGHN, baseball (1967)

16•NICOLE HAISLETT, swimming (1972)

15

1925 The third Madison Square Garden opened, with the Montreal Canadiens defeating the New York Americans. The New York City sports palace was the world's largest hockey arena at the time.

1963 Jim Brown of the Cleveland Browns ran for 125 yards on 28 carries in today's game against the Washington Redskins. His performance brought his season total to a record 1,863 yards — 103 yards more than a mile.

December 14, 1984: Eric Dickerson finishes the season with 2,105 yards rushing, an NFL record.

1993 New York Ranger goaltender Mike Richter tied a 54-year-old team record today. He won his 19th game in a row. By season's end, Mike will win a league-leading 42 games, and the Rangers will capture the Stanley Cup.

16

1984 Washington Redskins receiver Art Monk caught 11 passes to help the Redskins beat the St. Louis Cardinals, 29–27. Art's final catch gave him 106 on the season, an NFL record at the time.

1990 In Munich, Germany, tennis star Pete Sampras faced fellow American Brad Gilbert for the first Grand Slam Cup. Pete won the match in straight sets, 6–3, 6–4, 6–2. The $2 million first prize was the richest in tennis history. Pete earned about $74,000 per game!

1994 Shaquille O'Neal poured in 40 points as the Orlando Magic outlasted the Golden State Warriors in overtime, 131–128. But the game was also a battle of Hardaways. Orlando's Anfernee "Penny" Hardaway scored a career-high 38 points. That helped offset the 22 assists dished out by Golden State's Tim Hardaway.

17

1933 With three minutes left in the first NFL Championship Game, the Chicago Bears' Billy Karr scored a touchdown to nip the New York Giants, 23–21. Team founder George Halas, who was called "Papa Bear," will coach the team for 40 years and win seven NFL titles.

1979 There was no speed limit enforced at Edwards Air Force Base, in California, today. A vehicle with a rocket engine zipped along at 740 miles per hour! It was a record for a land vehicle with wheels. It was also the first time *any* land vehicle had broken the sound barrier.

1984 In the final minute of play, Miami Dolphin quarterback Dan Marino threw the winning touchdown pass to receiver Mark Clayton, to beat the Dallas Cowboys, 28–21. Dan threw four touchdown strikes in the game, raising his single-season total to 48 TD passes, an NFL record.

18

1932 The NFL held its first playoff in history, with the Chicago Bears taking on the Portsmouth (Ohio) Spartans. Wrigley Field was frozen, so the game was moved to an indoor arena. There was only enough room for an 80-yard field!

1949 The Philadelphia Eagles beat the Los Angeles Rams, 14–0, to win the NFL title for the second-straight year. Only 22,000 fans attended the game, which was played in the rain at Los Angeles Memorial Coliseum.

1983 "The Great One" got his 100th point of the season today. The Edmonton Oilers' Wayne Gretzky scored two goals and assisted on two others as the Oilers defeated the Winnipeg Jets, 7–5. Wayne's points raised his season total to 100 after just 34 games, setting an NHL record for the fastest 100 points in a season.

Birthdays

17•BOB OJEDA, baseball (1957)

18•ARANTXA SANCHEZ VICARIO, tennis (1971)

19•REGGIE WHITE, football (1961)

20•DUNCAN KENNEDY, luge (1967)

19

1989 The Charlotte Hornets defeated the Dallas Mavericks, 102–97, as Hornet point guard Muggsy Bogues dished out a season-high 18 assists. At 5' 3", Muggsy is the smallest player in NBA history.

1990 Bo Jackson of the Los Angeles Raiders was selected to play in the NFL Pro Bowl. Bo had played in major league baseball's All-Star Game back in July. He became the first pro athlete ever named as an All-Star in two sports.

December 17, 1984: Dan Marino sets an NFL record with his 48th touchdown pass of the season.

1992 Marshall University survived Youngstown State to win the Division I-AA national football championship. After trailing 28–0, Youngstown rallied to tie the game in the fourth quarter. But Marshall scored a field goal with 10 seconds left and won, 31–28.

20

1980 NBC television gave its football announcers the day off and aired a game without play-by-play or expert commentary. The move was not a hit with TV viewers. The announcers were back for the next game!

1985 Denis Potvin of the New York Islanders tallied his 916th career point, breaking Bobby Orr's NHL scoring record for defensemen. Denis played for the Islanders from 1973 to 1988. He was probably the best all-around defenseman in NHL history. He scored 310 goals and 1,052 points in his career and played on four Stanley Cup winners.

1987 San Francisco 49er receiver Jerry Rice made two touchdown catches in a 35–7 win over the Atlanta Falcons, to set an NFL record. Jerry had at least one touchdown reception in 12 straight games! (He will extend the record to 13 games.)

DECEMBER

21 **1926** The world champion St. Louis Cardinals traded their player-manager, Rogers Hornsby, to the New York Giants. Rogers was the greatest right-handed batter of all time. His career average of .358 is second only to Ty Cobb. He batted over .400 three times, including a record .424 in 1924.

1975 Playing in the final game of his amazing career, George Blanda of the Oakland Raiders became the first player in pro football history to score 2,000 career points. A quarterback and a place-kicker, George played until he was 48 years old! He played more seasons (26) in more games (340) and scored more points (2,002) than anyone else in NFL history.

1991 In a game against the Toronto Maple Leafs, Alexander Mogilny of the Buffalo Sabres tied an NHL record by scoring a goal just five seconds into the game!

22 **1985** Running back Roger Craig of the San Francisco 49ers became the first player in NFL history to gain at least 1,000 yards rushing and 1,000 yards receiving in a single season.

1991 Golfer Fred Couples won first prize in the Johnnie Walker World Championship, in Jamaica. Fred will be named PGA Player of the Year.

1994 In the first game since their big trade, the Golden State Warriors topped the Washington Bullets (now the Wizards), 107–87. The win put an end to Golden State's 10-game losing streak. The traded players performed well for their new teams: Tom Gugliotta had 18 points and 13 rebounds for the Warriors. Chris Webber had 14 points and 7 rebounds for the Bullets, but had to leave the game after he dislocated his shoulder.

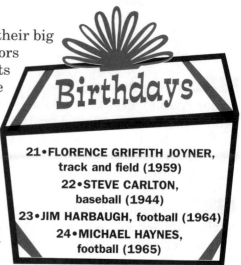

Birthdays

21•FLORENCE GRIFFITH JOYNER, track and field (1959)

22•STEVE CARLTON, baseball (1944)

23•JIM HARBAUGH, football (1964)

24•MICHAEL HAYNES, football (1965)

23

1921 Jigoro Kano of Japan, the inventor of judo, demonstrated the sport for the first time in the United States.

1972 The Pittsburgh Steelers trailed the Oakland Raiders, 7–6, in the first round of the AFC playoffs. On fourth down, with 22 seconds left, Steeler quarterback Terry Bradshaw zipped a pass that bounced off Raider safety Jack Tatum and into the hands of Steeler running back Franco Harris! Franco scooped up the ball just before it hit the ground and ran into the end zone for the winning touchdown!

December 23, 1993: Dominik Hasek gets his fourth shutout of the month.

1993 Buffalo Sabre goalie Dominik Hasek turned back 25 shots as the Sabres blanked the Montreal Canadiens, 5–0. The shutout was Dominik's fourth in December, making him the first goalie in the modern era to post four shutouts in one month.

24

1950 In their first season in the league, the Cleveland Browns won the NFL Championship! The Browns defeated the Los Angeles Rams in the title game, 30–28. Lou "The Toe" Groza made the difference by kicking a 16-yard field goal with 20 seconds to play.

1968 Center Garry Unger played in his first game on the way to a record. Garry, who played for several teams, will appear in 914 straight NHL games. The record will stand until 1987.

1995 Green Bay is once again known as Titletown! The Packers defeat the Pittsburgh Steelers, 24-19, on the final day of the regular season. The win clinches Green Bay's first outright NFC Central Division championship since 1972.

DECEMBER

25

1862 On Christmas Day, in the middle of the Civil War, two Union Army teams played a new sport. About 40,000 people watched as the two squads played a strange game called baseball, in Hilton Head, South Carolina. After the war ended, the soldiers brought the news of the sport back to their homes all over the country. They helped spread baseball's popularity.

1971 The longest game in NFL history was played today. It was an AFC playoff game between the Miami Dolphins and the Kansas City Chiefs. The game was decided after 22 minutes, 40 seconds of overtime, when Miami kicker Garo Yepremian booted a field goal to give the Dolphins a 27–24 win.

1984 New York Knick Bernard King electrified the crowd at Madison Square Garden with a franchise-record 60 points. But, the Knicks lost to the New Jersey Nets, 120–114.

26

1936 Track star Jesse Owens had won four gold medals at the Olympics less than eight months earlier. Today, he took on a race horse named Julio McGraw. A crowd of 3,000 spectators watched Jesse outrun the horse in the 100-yard dash. Amazing!

1991 Chuck Noll retired after 23 seasons as head coach of the Pittsburgh Steelers. Chuck, with 209 career victories, is one of only five coaches in NFL history with more than 200 wins. No other coach has won the Super Bowl as many times as Chuck. From 1974 to 1979, his teams won four Super Bowls.

1993 New York Ranger right wing Mike Gartner scored his 600th career goal in an 8–3 win over the New Jersey Devils. Mike became the sixth player in NHL history to reach 600 goals. By season's end, he will pass Bobby Hull for fifth place on the all-time scoring list.

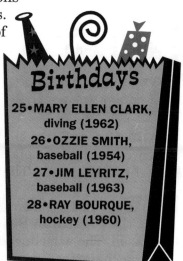

Birthdays

25 • MARY ELLEN CLARK, diving (1962)

26 • OZZIE SMITH, baseball (1954)

27 • JIM LEYRITZ, baseball (1963)

28 • RAY BOURQUE, hockey (1960)

27 **1991** In a game against Minnesota, All-Star guard Tim Hardaway of the Golden State Warriors missed all 17 of his field goal attempts, setting an NBA record. Teammate Chris Mullin came to the rescue, scoring 36 points in the Warriors' 106–102 victory.

1991 David Shula, 32, was hired by the Cincinnati Bengals as the youngest coach in NFL history. His father, Don, coaches the Miami Dolphins. The Shulas became the first father and son to coach in the NFL.

December 28, 1975: Roger Staubach fires deep ... and connects for a big score.

1992 Green Bay Packer receiver Sterling Sharpe made six catches in a 27–7 loss to the Minnesota Vikings, giving him an NFL record of 108 receptions for the season. The following season, Sterling caught 112 passes. In 1995, Detroit Lion receiver Herman Moore would catch an amazing 123 passes.

28 **1958** Called "The Greatest Game Ever Played," the 1958 NFL Championship Game between the Baltimore Colts and the New York Giants was tied at the end of regulation play. Eight minutes and 15 seconds into overtime, Colt fullback Alan Ameche scored on a one-yard plunge to give the Colts the victory.

1975 The Dallas Cowboys stunned the Minnesota Vikings, 17–14, in an NFC playoff game. With the Cowboys trailing and time running out, Dallas quarterback Roger Staubach reared back and threw a 50-yard pass, hoping receiver Drew Pearson would catch it. Somehow, Drew managed to grab it for the winning touchdown!

1993 The San Francisco Giants signed All-Star third baseman Matt Williams to a new contract today. The team agrees to pay Matt more than $30 million over five seasons.

29

1961 The Philadelphia Warriors defeated the Los Angeles Lakers, 123–118, as Wilt Chamberlain poured in 60 points. It was the seventh-straight game in which Wilt scored at least 50 points. He will later set the current record of 100 points in a game.

1978 There was nothing out of the ordinary in today's Gator Bowl between Clemson and Ohio State Universities . . . until Buckeye coach Woody Hayes punched a Clemson lineman. Coach Hayes was fired for striking an opposing player. He had won 238 games and three national championships during his coaching career. (Woody's Ohio State team lost today's game, 17–15.)

1994 The Atlanta Hawks' 127–121 overtime victory against the San Antonio Spurs was extra sweet for Hawk coach Lenny Wilkens. It was his 938th win. The victory tied him with Red Auerbach as the winningest coach of all time. He broke the record the next week.

30

1936 At a time when basketball players were taught to use a two-handed set shot, Hank Luisetti of Stanford University showed off a new shot: the running one-hander. Stanford had come east to play Long Island University, winner of 43 straight games. Stanford beat the Pioneers, 45–31. Hank scored 15 points.

1990 Scott Skiles of the Orlando Magic handed out 30 assists in today's 155–116 win over the Denver Nuggets, setting an NBA record.

1990 Detroit Lion running back Barry Sanders finished the season with 1,304 yards rushing, tops in the NFL. Barry became the first Lion to win the rushing title since Byron "Whizzer" White did it in 1940. Whizzer will go on to become an associate justice on the United States Supreme Court.

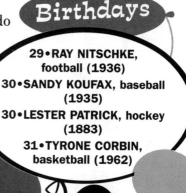

Birthdays

29 • **RAY NITSCHKE,** football (1936)

30 • **SANDY KOUFAX, baseball** (1935)

30 • **LESTER PATRICK, hockey** (1883)

31 • **TYRONE CORBIN,** basketball (1962)

DECEMBER

31 **1967** Green Bay Packer guard Jerry Kramer made the block of a lifetime in today's NFL Championship Game. His play allowed Packer quarterback Bart Starr to dive into the end zone to score the winning touchdown with 13 seconds remaining in the game. Green Bay won the "Ice Bowl," 21–17. (The game is known as the Ice Bowl because, at game time, the temperature was an icy 13 degrees below!)

1985 *Oops!* Jockey Jorge Velasquez made a big mistake at Aqueduct Racetrack, in New York City. During a race, Jorge dug his heels in and got his horse to run as fast as he could. Jorge thought he was near the finish line. He wasn't. The finish line was still a mile away! By the time he neared the finish line, his horse was pooped.

December 31, 1988: Mario Lemieux scores five goals in a game.

1988 A five-goal performance by Pittsburgh's Mario Lemieux made NHL history: The Penguin center scored one of each type of goal possible — even strength, power play, shorthanded, penalty shot, and empty net. (The NHL record for goals in a game is seven, set by Joe Malone of the Quebec Bulldogs in 1920.)

1995 The Green Bay Packers defeated the Atlanta Falcons, 37–20, in the first round of the NFC playoffs. The following day, Packer quarterback Brett Favre won the first of his back-to-back NFL MVP awards. In 1995, Favre led the league with 38 TD passes and 4,413 passing yards.

Photo Credits

UPI/BETTMANN: 13, 15, 17, 19, 21, 23, 25, 26, 29, 31, 33, 35, 37, 39, 41, 42, 45, 47, 51, 53, 55, 59, 63, 65, 67, 69, 73, 77, 79, 83, 85, 95, 97, 99, 101, 103, 107, 108, 113, 115, 117, 119, 121, 123, 125, 127, 129, 131, 135, 137, 139, 141, 149, 151, 153, 158, 163, 165, 169, 177, 179, 181, 183, 185, 187, 191, 195, 199, 201, 203, 205, 207

SPORTS ILLUSTRATED: 11 (Neil Leifer), 49 (Bill Frakes), 75 (Jerry Wachter), 87 (Bill Smith), 142 (Heinz Kluetmeier), 145 (Ronald C. Modra), 147, 159 (John Biever), 167, 173, 175 (Brad Mangin), 189

AP/WIDE WORLD PHOTOS: 9, 57, 61, 81, 89, 91, 92, 105, 111, 133, 155, 157, 171, 193, 197

NATHANIEL S. BUTLER/NBA PHOTOS: 71

DAVE BLACK: 108

C. ANDERSEN/BBS: 203